THE SREBRENICA GENOCIDE : ABOMINABLE ATROCITIES IN OUR LIFETIME

Three years before the July 1995 Srebrenica Genocide, Serbs torched Bosniak/Bosnian Muslim villages and killed at least 3,166 Bosniaks around Srebrenica. In 1993, the UN described the besieged situation in Srebrenica as a "slow-motion process of genocide." In July 1995, Serbs forcibly expelled 25,000 Bosniaks, brutally raped many women and girls, and systematically killed 8,000+ men and boys (DNA confirmed).

It is clear who the perpetrators and who the victims were during the Bosnian war. To put things into perspective: During the war, not even one Serb city was under the siege by Bosniak forces; in fact, majority of Serb civilian casualties were killed by the Serbian army commanded by Gen. Ratko Mladic in the process of sniping and shelling multiethnic Bosnian cities like Sarajevo and Tuzla. Serb people and Serb culture were not deliberately targeted for ethnic cleansing, rape, siege, shelling, and destruction in Bosnia; it was the Serb project of "Greater Serbia", modeled on a Nazi policy of ethnic purification, that inflicted tremendous suffering on the Bosniak people between 1992 and 1995.

The Bosnian War was an international armed conflict that took place in Bosnia and Herzegovina between April 1992 and December 1995. The war involved several sides. The main belligerents were the forces of the Republic of Bosnia and Herzegovina and those of the self-proclaimed Bosnian Serb and Bosnian Croat entities within Bosnia and Herzegovina -- 'Republika Srpska' and 'Herzeg-Bosnia'. Both 'para-states' enjoyed substantial political and military backing (overall control) from Serbia and Croatia respectively. NATO was involved in air-strikes against the Serbs.

The Hague Tribunal: The Office of the Prosecutor of the International Criminal Tribunal at the Hague proved -- that the Bosnian war was NOT a 'civil war' but an international armed conflict involving Serbia, Bosnia, Croatia and NATO.

Theodor Meron, the presiding judge of the ICTY Appeals Chamber, stated:

By seeking to eliminate a part of the Bosnian Muslims, the Bosnian Serb forces committed genocide. They targeted for extinction the 40,000 Bosnian Muslims living in Srebrenica, a group which was emblematic of the Bosnian Muslims in general. They stripped all the male Muslim prisoners, military and civilian, elderly and young, of their personal belongings and identification, and deliberately and methodically killed them solely on the basis of their identity.

I had successfully studied the cases and situations involving Bosnia-Herzegovina and other republics of the former Yugoslavia for the subject of Public International Law for my final year study for the course of the Bachelor of Laws (Hons) in 1997-1998 and dedicate this book to my parents, siblings, friends, relatives and our brothers and sisters of Bosnia-Herzegovina, especially the innocent victims of armed conflict/war and genocide. May we achieve and attain our dreams!

The Srebrenica massacre, also known as the Srebrenica genocide (Bosnian: Masakar u Srebrenici; Genocid u Srebrenici), was the genocidal killing, in July 1995, of more than 8,000 Bosnian Muslim/Bosniaks, mainly men and boys, in and around the town of Srebrenica during the Bosnian War. According to the Potocari Memorial Center Preliminary List of Missing Persons from Srebrenica '95, the number of victims stood at 8373.

The killings were perpetrated by units of the Bosnian Serb Army of Republika Srpska (VRS) under the command of General Ratko Mladić. The Scorpions, a paramilitary unit from Serbia, who had been part of the Serbian Interior Ministry until 1991, also participated in the massacre. In April 1993 the United Nations had declared the besieged enclave of Srebrenica—in the Drina Valley of northeastern Bosnia—a "safe area" under UN protection. However, in July 1995, UNPROFOR's 370 Dutchbat soldiers in Srebrenica failed to prevent the town's capture by the VRS — and the subsequent massacre.

In 2004, in a unanimous ruling on the case of Prosecutor v. Krstić, the Appeals Chamber of the International Criminal Tribunal for the former Yugoslavia (ICTY), located in the Hague, ruled that the massacre of the enclave's male inhabitants constituted genocide, a crime under international law. The ruling was also upheld by the International Court of Justice (ICJ) in 2007. The forcible transfer of between 25,000 and 30,000 Bosniak women, children and elderly which accompanied the massacre was found to constitute genocide, when accompanied with the killings and separation of the men.

In 2005, Kofi Annan, then Secretary-General of the United Nations described the mass murder as the worst crime on European soil since the Second World War, and in a message to the tenth anniversary commemoration of the massacre, he wrote that, while blame lay "first and foremost with those who planned and carried out the massacre and those who assisted and harboured them", the UN had "made serious errors of judgement, rooted in a philosophy of impartiality", describing Srebrenica as a tragedy that would haunt the history of the UN forever.

In 2006, in the Bosnian Genocide case held before the International Court of Justice, Serbia and Montenegro was cleared of direct responsibility for, or complicity in, the massacre, but was found responsible for not doing enough to prevent the genocide and not prosecuting those responsible, in breach of the Genocide Convention. The Preliminary List of People Missing or Killed in Srebrenica compiled by the Bosnian Federal Commission of Missing Persons contains 8,373 names. As of July 2012, 6,838 genocide victims have been identified through DNA analysis of body parts recovered from mass graves; as of July 2013, 6,066 victims have been buried at the Memorial Centre of Potočari.

In April 2013, Serbian President Tomislav Nikolić officially apologised for the massacre, although he stopped short of calling it genocide. In 2013 and 2014, the Netherlands was found liable in its own supreme court and in the Hague district court of failing in its duty to prevent more than 300 of the deaths. On 8 July 2015, Russia vetoed, by request of the Republika Srpska and Serbia, a UN resolution condemning the Srebrenica massacre as genocide, Serbia calling the resolution "anti-Serb". On 9 July 2015, both Members of the European Parliament (EP) and House of Representatives of the U.S. Congress adopted resolutions on Srebrenica reaffirming the description of the crime as genocide.

Contents

Background

Conflict in eastern Bosnia

1992 ethnic cleansing campaign

Fate of Bosniak villages

Struggle for Srebrenica 1992–1993

Starvation in Srebrenica 1992–1995

Organization of UNPROFOR and UNPF

The Srebrenica "safe area"

April 1993: the Security Council declares Srebrenica a "safe area"

Serb refusal to demilitarise around Srebrenica

Early 1995: the situation in the Srebrenica "safe area" deteriorates

4 June and 6–11 July 1995: Serb take-over of Srebrenica

Massacre

The increasing concentration of refugees in Potočari

Crimes committed in Potočari

Separation and murder of Bosniak men and boys in Potočari

Rape and abuse of civilians

Deportation of women

Column of Bosniak men

Other groups

Tuzla column departs

Ambush at Kamenica Hill

Sandići massacre

Trek to Mount Udrc

Snagovo ambush

Approaching the frontline

Breakthrough at Baljkovica

Baljkovica corridor

Arrival at Tuzla

After the closure of the corridor

Plan to execute the men of Srebrenica

Mass executions

Morning of 13 July: Jadar River

Afternoon of 13 July: Cerska Valley

Late afternoon of 13 July: Kravica

13–14 July: Tišća

14 July: Grbavci and Orahovac

14–15 July: Petkovići

14–16 July: Branjevo

14–17 July: Kozluk

13–18 July: Bratunac-Konjević Polje road

18–19 July: Nezuk-Baljkovica frontline

20–22 July: Meces area

After the massacre

Wanderers

Reburials in the secondary mass graves

Greek Volunteers controversy

End of the war

Post-war developments

1995: indictment of Radovan Karadžić and Ratko Mladić

1999 UN Secretary-General's report

2002 Dutch government report

2002 First Republika Srpska report

2003: Srebrenica Genocide Memorial

2004: Second Republika Srpska report and official apology

2005 Release of Scorpions massacre video

2005 U.S. Congress and other resolutions

2005 Potočari Memorial bomb plot

2005 UN Secretary-General's message to the 10th anniversary commemoration

2005 Perpetrators named

2006 Discoveries of further mass graves

2006 Suppressed list of perpetrators in positions of authority published

2006 Dutch Srebrenica medal controversy

2007 Arrest of Zdravko Tolimir

2008 Arrest of Radovan Karadžić

2009 EU Parliament resolution

2010 and 2012 Serbia's official apologies

2010 Second Republika Srpska report revision

2013 Supreme Court of the Netherlands judgement

2015 Russia vetoes UN resolution

DNA analysis

Legal proceedings

International Criminal Tribunal for the former Yugoslavia

International Court of Justice

National courts

Serbia

Bosnia and Herzegovina

Netherlands

Analyses

Role of Bosnian forces on the ground

Dispute regarding Serb casualties around Srebrenica

Claim that the planning of mass executions in Srebrenica defies military logic

Dutchbat

Claims of problems in the UNPROFOR chain of command above "Dutchbat"

Claims and retraction by retired NATO SACLANT

Criticism of the 1995 UN Special Representative for the former Yugoslavia

Denial and scepticism

Individuals and groups who have challenged or denied the events at Srebrenica as genocide

Conflict in eastern Bosnia

The multiethnic Socialist Republic of Bosnia and Herzegovina was mainly inhabited by Bosnian Muslim/Bosniaks (44 percent), Orthodox Serbs (31 percent) and Catholic Croats (17 percent). Following a declaration of national sovereignty on 15 October 1991 as the former Yugoslavia began to disintegrate, a referendum for independence was held on 29 February 1992. The result, in favour of independence, was rejected by the political representatives of the Bosnian Serbs who had boycotted the referendum. The Republic of Bosnia and Herzegovina was formally recognised by the European Community on 6 April 1992, and by the United States the following day. Following the declaration of independence, Bosnian Serb forces, supported by the Serbian government of Slobodan Milošević and the Yugoslav People's Army (JNA), attacked the Republic of Bosnia and Herzegovina in order to unify and secure Serb territory. A fierce struggle for territorial control ensued, accompanied by the ethnic cleansing of the non-Serb population from areas under Serb control; in particular, the Bosniak population of Eastern Bosnia, near the border with Serbia.

1992 ethnic cleansing campaign

The predominantly Bosniak area of Central Podrinje (the region around Srebrenica) had a primary strategic importance to Serbs, as without it there would be no territorial integrity within their new political entity of Republika Srpska. They thus proceeded with the ethnic cleansing of Bosniaks from Bosniak ethnic territories in Eastern Bosnia and Central Podrinje. In the words of the ICTY judgement:

Once towns and villages were securely in their hands, the Serb forces – the military, the police, the paramilitaries and, sometimes, even Serb villagers –

applied the same pattern: Muslim houses and apartments were systematically ransacked or burnt down, Muslim villagers were rounded up or captured and, in the process, sometimes beaten or killed. Men and women were separated, with many of the men detained in the former KP Dom prison.

In neighbouring Bratunac, Bosniaks were either killed or forced to flee to Srebrenica, resulting in 1,156 deaths, according to Bosnian government data. Thousands of Bosniaks were also killed in Foča, Zvornik, Cerska and Snagovo.

Fate of Bosniak villages

The Bosnian Institute in the UK has published a list of 296 villages destroyed by Serb forces around Srebrenica during the first three months of war (April – June 1992):

More than three years before the 1995 Srebrenica genocide, Bosnian Serb nationalists – with the logistical, moral and financial support of Serbia and the Yugoslav People's Army (JNA) – destroyed 296 predominantly Bosniak villages in the region around Srebrenica, forcibly uprooting some 70,000 Bosniaks from their homes and systematically massacring at least 3,166 Bosniaks (documented deaths) including many women, children and elderly.

According to the Naser Orić trial judgement:

Between April 1992 and March 1993, the town of Srebrenica and the villages in the area held by Bosniak were constantly subjected to Serb military assaults, including artillery attacks, sniper fire, as well as occasional bombing from aircraft. Each onslaught followed a similar pattern. Serb soldiers and paramilitaries surrounded a Bosnian Muslim village or hamlet, called upon the population to surrender their weapons, and then began with indiscriminate shelling and shooting. In most cases, they then entered the village or hamlet, expelled or killed the population, who offered no significant resistance, and destroyed their homes. During this period, Srebrenica was subjected to indiscriminate shelling from all directions on a daily basis. Potočari in particular was a daily target for Serb artillery and infantry because it was a sensitive point in the defence line around Srebrenica. Other Bosnian Muslim settlements were routinely attacked as well. All this resulted in a great number of refugees and casualties.

Struggle for Srebrenica 1992–1993

Serb military and paramilitary forces from the area and neighbouring parts of eastern Bosnia and Serbia gained control of Srebrenica for several weeks in early 1992, killing and expelling Bosniak civilians. In May 1992, Bosnian government forces under the leadership of Orić recaptured the town.

Over the remainder of 1992, offensives by Bosnian government forces from Srebrenica increased the area under their control, and by January 1993 they had linked with Bosniak-held Žepa to the south and Cerska to the west. At this time, the Srebrenica enclave had reached its peak size of 900 square kilometres (350 sq miles), although it was never linked to the main area of Bosnian-government controlled land in the west and remained, in the words of the ICTY, "a vulnerable island amid Serb-controlled territory".

Over the next few months, the Serb military captured the villages of Konjević Polje and Cerska, severing the link between Srebrenica and Žepa and reducing the size of the Srebrenica enclave to 150 square kilometres. Bosniak residents of the outlying areas converged on the town of Srebrenica and its population swelled to between 50,000 and 60,000 people.

General Philippe Morillon of France, Commander of the United Nations Protection Force (UNPROFOR), visited Srebrenica in March 1993. By then, the town was overcrowded and siege conditions prevailed. There was almost no running water as the advancing Serb forces had destroyed the town's water supplies; people relied on makeshift generators for electricity. Food, medicine and other essentials were extremely scarce. Before leaving, General Morillon told the panicked residents of Srebrenica at a public gathering that the town was under the protection of the UN and that he would never abandon them.

Between March and April 1993 several thousand Bosniaks were evacuated from Srebrenica under the auspices of the UN High Commissioner for Refugees (UNHCR). The evacuations were opposed by the Bosnian government in Sarajevo as contributing to the ethnic cleansing of predominantly Bosniak territory.

The Serb authorities remained intent on capturing the enclave. On 13 April 1993, the Serbs told the UNHCR representatives that they would attack the town within two days unless the Bosniaks surrendered and agreed to be evacuated. The Bosniaks refused to surrender.

Starvation in Srebrenica 1992–1995

A former Serb soldier of the "Red Berets" unit described the tactics used to starve and kill the besieged population of Srebrenica:

"It was almost like a game, a cat-and-mouse hunt. But of course we greatly outnumbered the Muslims, so in almost all cases, we were the hunters and they were the prey. We needed them to surrender, but how do you get someone to surrender in a war like this? You starve them to death. So very quickly we realised that it wasn't really weapons being smuggled into Srebrenica that we should worry about, but food. They were truly starving in there, so they would send people out to steal cattle or gather crops, and our job was to find and kill them... No prisoners. Well, yes, if we thought they had useful information, we might keep them alive until we got it out of them, but in the end, no prisoners. The local people became quite indignant, so sometimes we would keep someone alive to hand over to them [to kill] just to keep them happy."

When Australian journalist Tony Birtley visited the besieged Srebrenica in March 1993, he took footage of Bosniak civilians starving to death.

The judgment of the Hague Tribunal in the case of Naser Oric found that:

"Bosnian Serb forces controlling the access roads were not allowing international humanitarian aid – most importantly, food and medicine – to reach Srebrenica. As a consequence, there was a constant and serious shortage of food causing starvation to peak in the winter of 1992/1993. Numerous people died or were in an extremely emaciated state due to malnutrition. Bosnian Muslim fighters and their families, however, were provided with food rations from existing storage facilities. The most disadvantaged group among the Bosnian Muslims were the refugees, who usually lived on the streets and without shelter, in freezing temperatures. Only in November and December 1992, did two UN convoys with humanitarian aid reach the enclave, and this despite Bosnian Serb obstruction."

Organization of UNPROFOR and UNPF

Main article: United Nations Protection Force

In April 1995, UNPROFOR became the name used only for the Bosnia regional command of the now renamed, United Nations Peace Forces (UNPF).

The 2011 report Srebrenica: a 'safe' area said that "On 12 June 1995 a new command was created under UNPF, it had "12,500 British, French and Dutch troops equipped with tanks and high calibre artillery in order to increase the effectiveness and the credibility of the peacekeeping operation".

Furthermore, it said, "In the UNPROFOR chain of command, Dutchbat occupied the fourth tier, with the sector commanders occupying the third tier. The fourth tier primarily had an operational task. Within this structure, Dutchbat was expected to operate as an independent unit with its own logistic arrangements. Dutchbat was dependent on the UNPROFOR organization to some extent for crucial supplies such as fuel. For the rest, it was expected to obtain its supplies from the Netherlands. From an organizational point of view, the battalion had two lifelines: UNPROFOR and the Royal Netherlands Army. Dutchbat had been assigned responsibility for the Srebrenica Safe Area. Neither UNPROFOR nor Bosnia-Hercegovina paid much attention to Srebrenica, however. Srebrenica was situated in eastern Bosnia, which was geographically and mentally far removed from Sarajevo and Zagreb. The rest of the world was focused on the fight for Sarajevo and the peace process. As a Safe Area, Srebrenica only occasionally managed to attract the attention of the world press or the UN Security Council. That is why the Dutch troops there remained of secondary importance, in operational and logistic terms, for so long; and why the importance of the enclave in the battle for domination between the Bosnian Serbs and Bosnian Muslims failed to be recognised for so long".

The Srebrenica "safe area"

Areas of control in Bosnia and Herzegovina in September 1994; eastern Bosnian enclaves near the Serbian border

April 1993: the Security Council declares Srebrenica a "safe area"

On 16 April 1993, the United Nations Security Council passed Resolution 819, which demanded that: "all parties and others concerned treat Srebrenica and its surroundings as a safe area which should be free from any armed attack or any other hostile act". On 18 April 1993, the first group of UNPROFOR troops arrived in Srebrenica. On 8 May 1993 agreement was reached of demilitarization of Srebrenica. According to UN reports "General [Sefer] Halilović and General [Ratko] Mladić agreed on measures covering the whole of the Srebrenica enclave and the adjacent enclave of Žepa. Under the terms of the new agreement, Bosniak forces within the enclave would hand over their weapons, ammunition and mines to UNPROFOR, after which Serb "heavy weapons and units that constituted a menace to the demilitarised zones which will have been established in Žepa and Srebrenica will be withdrawn." Unlike the earlier agreement, the agreement of 8 May stated specifically that Srebrenica was to be considered a "demilitarised zone", as referred to in article 60 of the Protocol Additional to the Geneva Conventions of 12 August 1949, and relating to the Protection of Victims of International Armed Conflicts (Protocol I)."

Between 1,000 and 2,000 soldiers from three of the VRS Drina Corps Brigades were deployed around the enclave, equipped with tanks, armoured vehicles, artillery and mortars. The 28th Mountain Division of the Army of the Republic of Bosnia and Herzegovina (ARBiH) remaining in the enclave was neither well organised nor equipped: a firm command structure and communications system was lacking and some soldiers carried old hunting rifles or no weapons at all. Few had proper uniforms.

From the outset, both parties to the conflict violated the "safe area" agreement. Lieutenant-Colonel Thomas Karremans (the Dutchbat

Commander) testified to the ICTY that his personnel were prevented from returning to the enclave by Serb forces and that equipment and ammunition were also prevented from getting in. Bosniaks in Srebrenica complained of attacks by Serb soldiers, while to the Serbs it appeared that Bosnian government forces in Srebrenica were using the "safe area" as a convenient base from which to launch counter-offensives against the Army of the Republika Srpska (VRS) and that UNPROFOR was failing to take any action to prevent it. General Sefer Halilović admitted that ARBiH helicopters had flown in violation of the no-fly zone and that he had personally dispatched eight helicopters with ammunition for the 28th Division.

Serb refusal to demilitarise around Srebrenica

A Security Council mission led by Diego Arria arrived in Srebrenica on 25 April 1993 and, in their subsequent report to the U.N., condemned the Serbs for perpetrating "a slow-motion process of genocide." The mission then stated that "Serb forces must withdraw to points from which they cannot attack, harass or terrorise the town. UNPROFOR should be in a position to determine the related parameters. The mission believes, as does UNPROFOR, that the actual 4.5 km by 0.5 km decided as a safe area should be greatly expanded." Specific instructions from United Nations Headquarters in New York stated that UNPROFOR should not be too zealous in searching for Bosniak weapons and, later, that the Serbs should withdraw their heavy weapons before the Bosniaks gave up their weapons. The Serbs never did withdraw their heavy weapons.

Early 1995: the situation in the Srebrenica "safe area" deteriorates

By early 1995, fewer and fewer supply convoys were making it through to the enclave. The situation in Srebrenica and in other enclaves had deteriorated into lawless violence as prostitution among young Muslim girls, theft and black marketeering proliferated. The already meager resources of the civilian population dwindled further and even the UN forces started running dangerously low on food, medicine, ammunition and fuel, eventually being forced to start patrolling the enclave on foot. Dutchbat soldiers who went out of the area on leave were not allowed to return and their number dropped from 600 to 400 men. In March and April, the Dutch soldiers noticed a build-up of Serb forces near two of the observation posts, "OP Romeo" and "OP Quebec".

In March 1995, Radovan Karadžić, President of the Republika Srpska (RS), despite pressure from the international community to end the war and ongoing efforts to negotiate a peace agreement, issued a directive to the VRS concerning the long-term strategy of the VRS forces in the enclave. The directive, known as "Directive 7", specified that the VRS was to:

Complete the physical separation of Srebrenica from Žepa as soon as possible, preventing even communication between individuals in the two enclaves. By planned and well-thought out combat operations, create an unbearable situation of total insecurity with no hope of further survival or life for the inhabitants of Srebrenica.

By mid-1995, the humanitarian situation of the Bosniak civilians and military personnel in the enclave was catastrophic. In May, following orders, Orić and his staff left the enclave by helicopter to Tuzla, leaving senior officers in command of the 28th Division. In late June and early July, the 28th Division issued a series of reports including urgent pleas for the humanitarian corridor to the enclave to be reopened. When this failed, Bosniak civilians began dying from starvation. On Friday, 7 July the mayor of Srebrenica reported 8 residents had died of starvation.

4 June and 6–11 July 1995 : Serb take-over of Srebrenica

On 4 June 1995, the commander of the UN forces in former Yugoslavia, general Bernard Janvier - from France - secretly met with Ratko Mladić to obtain the release of hostages, many of whom were French. Mladić demanded of Janvier that there would be no more air strikes.

The Serb offensive against Srebrenica began in earnest on 6 July 1995. In the following days, the five UNPROFOR observation posts in the southern part of the enclave fell one by one in the face of the Bosnian Serb advance. Some of the Dutch soldiers retreated into the enclave after their posts were attacked, but the crews of the other observation posts surrendered into Serb custody. Simultaneously, the defending Bosnian forces came under heavy fire and were pushed back towards the town. Once the southern perimeter began to collapse, about 4,000 Bosniak residents who had been living in a Swedish housing complex for refugees nearby fled north into the town of Srebrenica. Dutch soldiers reported that the advancing Serbs were "cleansing" the houses in the southern part of the enclave.

A Dutch YPR-765 as used at Srebrenica

On 8 July, a Dutch YPR-765 armoured vehicle took fire from the Serbs and withdrew. A group of Bosniaks demanded that the armoured vehicle stay to defend them, and established a makeshift brigade to prevent its retreat. As the armoured vehicle continued to withdraw, a Bosniak farmer who was manning the barricade threw a hand grenade onto it and subsequently killed Dutch soldier Raviv van Renssen.   Late on 9 July 1995, emboldened by early successes and little resistance from the largely demilitarised Bosniaks as well as the absence of any significant reaction from the international community, the President of the Republika Srpska, Radovan Karadžić, issued a new order authorising the 1,500-strong VRS Drina Corps to capture the town of Srebrenica.

The following morning (10 July 1995), Lieutenant-Colonel Karremans made urgent requests for air support from NATO to defend Srebrenica as crowds filled the streets, some of whom carried weapons. VRS tanks were approaching the town, and NATO airstrikes on these began on the afternoon of 11 July 1995. NATO bombers attempted to attack VRS artillery locations outside the town but poor visibility forced NATO to cancel this operation. Further NATO air attacks were cancelled after VRS threats to bomb the UN's Potočari compound, to kill Dutch and French military hostages and to attack surrounding locations where 20,000 to 30,000 civilian refugees were situated.

Late in the afternoon of 11 July, General Mladić, accompanied by General Živanović (then-Commander of the Drina Corps), General Krstić (then-Deputy Commander and Chief of Staff of the Drina Corps) and other VRS officers, took a triumphant walk through the deserted streets of the town of Srebrenica.

In the evening,[67] Lieutenant-Colonel Thom Karremans was filmed drinking a toast with General Mladić during the bungled negotiations on the fate of the civilian population grouped in Potočari.

Massacre

The two highest ranking Serb politicians from Bosnia and Herzegovina, Karadžić and Momčilo Krajišnik, both indicted for genocide, were warned by military commander General Mladić (also indicted on genocide charges) that their plans could not be realised without committing genocide. Mladić said:

People are not little stones, or keys in someone's pocket, that can be moved from one place to another just like that.... Therefore, we cannot precisely arrange for only Serbs to stay in one part of the country while removing others painlessly. I do not know how Mr. Krajišnik and Mr. Karadžić will explain that to the world. That is genocide.

The increasing concentration of refugees in Potočari

Headquarters in Potočari for soldiers under United Nations command; "Dutchbat" had 370 soldiers in Srebrenica during the massacre. The building was a disused battery factory.

By the evening of 11 July 1995, approximately 20,000 to 25,000 Bosniak refugees from Srebrenica were gathered in Potočari, seeking protection within the UNPROFOR Dutchbat headquarters. Several thousand had pressed inside the compound itself, while the rest were spread throughout the neighbouring factories and fields. Though the vast majority were women, children, elderly or disabled, 63 witnesses estimated that there were at least 300 men inside the perimeter of the UNPROFOR compound and between 600 and 900 men in the crowd outside. UNPROFOR Dutchbat soldiers [on site] claimed their base was full.

Conditions in Potočari included "little food or water available" and sweltering heat. One UNPROFOR Dutchbat officer described the scene as follows:

They were panicked, they were scared, and they were pressing each other against the soldiers, my soldiers, the UN soldiers that tried to calm them. People that fell were trampled on. It was a chaotic situation.

On 12 July, the United Nations Security Council, in Resolution 1004, expressed concern at the humanitarian situation in Potočari, which also condemned the offensive by Bosnian Serb forces and demanded immediate withdrawal.

On 13 July, the Dutch forces expelled five Bosniak refugees from the United Nations compound despite knowing that men outside the compound were being killed and abused.

Crimes committed in Potočari

On 12 July 1995, as the day wore on, the refugees in the compound could see VRS soldiers setting houses and haystacks on fire. Throughout the afternoon, Serb soldiers mingled in the crowd and summary executions of men occurred. In the late morning of 12 July 1995 a witness saw a pile of 20 to 30 bodies heaped up behind the Transport Building in Potočari, alongside a tractor-like machine. Another testified that he saw a soldier slay a child with a knife in the middle of a crowd of expellees. He also said that he saw Serb soldiers execute more than a hundred Bosnian Muslim men in the area behind the Zinc Factory and then load their bodies onto a truck, although the number and nature of the murders stand in contrast to other evidence on the Trial Record which indicates that the killings in Potočari were sporadic in nature. Soldiers were picking people out of the crowd and taking them away. A witness recounted how three brothers – one merely a child and the others in their teens – were taken out in the night. When the boys' mother went looking for them, she found them stark naked and with their throats slit.

That night, a Dutchbat medical orderly witnessed two Serb soldiers raping a young woman.

One survivor described the murder of a baby and the rape of women occurring in the close vicinity of Dutch U.N. peacekeepers who did nothing to prevent it. According to the survivor, a Serb told a mother to make her child stop crying, and when it continued to cry he took it and slit its throat, after which he laughed. Stories about rapes and killings spread through the crowd and the terror in the camp escalated. Several individuals were so terrified that they committed suicide by hanging themselves.

One of the survivors, Zarfa Turkovic, described the horrors of rapes as follows: "Two [Serb soldiers] took her legs and raised them up in the air, while the third began raping her. Four of them were taking turns on her. People were silent, no one moved. She was screaming and yelling and begging them to stop. They put a rag into her mouth and then we just heard silent sobs...."

Separation and murder of Bosniak men and boys in Potočari

From the morning of 12 July, Serb forces began gathering men and boys from the refugee population in Potočari and holding them in separate locations, and as the refugees began boarding the buses headed north towards Bosniak-held territory, Serb soldiers separated out men of military age who were trying to clamber aboard. Occasionally, younger and older men were stopped as well (some as young as 14 or 15). These men were taken to a building in Potočari referred to as the "White House". As early as the evening of 12 July 1995, Major Franken of the Dutchbat heard that no men were arriving with the women and children at their destination in Kladanj. At this time, the UNHCR Director of Operations, Peter Walsh, was dispatched to Srebrenica by the UNHCR Chief of Mission, Damaso Feci, to evaluate what emergency aid could be provided rapidly. Peter Walsh and his team arrived at Gostilj, just outside Srebrenica, in the early afternoon only to be turned away by VRS forces. Despite claiming freedom of movement rights, the UNHCR team was not allowed to proceed and was forced to head back north to Bijelina.

Throughout this time, Peter Walsh relayed reports back to UNHCR in Zagreb about the unfolding situation including witnessing the enforced movement and abuse of Muslim men and boys and the sound of summary executions taking place.

On 13 July 1995, Dutchbat troops witnessed definite signs that the Serb soldiers were murdering some of the Bosniak men who had been separated. For example, Corporal Vaasen saw two soldiers take a man behind the "White House", heard a shot and saw the two soldiers reappear alone. Another Dutchbat officer saw Serb soldiers murder an unarmed man with a single gunshot to the head and heard gunshots 20–40 times an hour throughout the afternoon. When the Dutchbat soldiers told Colonel Joseph Kingori, a United Nations Military Observer (UNMO) in the Srebrenica area, that men were being taken behind the "White House" and not coming back, Colonel Kingori went to investigate. He heard gunshots as he approached, but was stopped by Serb soldiers before he could find out what was going on.

Some of the executions were carried out at night under arc lights, and industrial bulldozers then pushed the bodies into mass graves. According to evidence collected from Bosniaks by French policeman Jean-René Ruez, some were buried alive; he also heard testimony describing Serb forces killing and torturing refugees at will, streets littered with corpses, people committing suicide to avoid having their noses, lips and ears chopped off, and adults being forced to watch the soldiers kill their children.

Rape and abuse of civilians

Many women and girls suffered rape and sexual abuse and other forms of torture. According to the testimony of Zumra Šehomerovic :

The Serbs began at a certain point to take girls and young women out of the group of refugees. They were raped. The rapes often took place under the eyes of others and sometimes even under the eyes of the children of the mother. A Dutch soldier stood by and he simply looked around with a Walkman on his head. He did not react at all to what was happening. It did not happen just before my eyes, for I saw that personally, but also before the eyes of us all. The Dutch soldiers walked around everywhere. It is impossible that they did not see it.

There was a woman with a small baby a few months old. A Chetnik told the mother that the child must stop crying. When the child did not stop crying, he snatched the child away and cut its throat. Then he laughed. There was a Dutch soldier there who was watching. He did not react at all.

I saw yet more frightful things. For example, there was a girl, she must have been about nine years old. At a certain moment some Chetniks recommended to her brother that he rape the girl. He did not do it and I also think that he could not have done it for he was still just a child. Then they murdered that young boy. I have personally seen all that. I really want to emphasize that all this happened in the immediate vicinity of the base. In the same way I also saw other people who were murdered. Some of them had their throats cut. Others were beheaded.

Testimony of Ramiza Gurdić:

I saw how a young boy of about ten was killed by Serbs in Dutch uniform. This happened in front of my own eyes. The mother sat on the ground and her young son sat beside her. The young boy was placed on his mother's lap. The young boy was killed. His head was cut off. The body remained on the lap of the mother. The Serbian soldier placed the head of the young boy on his knife and showed it to everyone. ... I saw how a pregnant woman was slaughtered. There were Serbs who stabbed her in the stomach, cut her open and took two small children out of her stomach and then beat them to death on the ground. I saw this with my own eyes.

Testimony of Kada Hotić:

There was a young woman with a baby on the way to the bus. The baby cried and a Serbian soldier told her that she had to make sure that the baby was quiet. Then the soldier took the child from the mother and cut its throat. I do not know whether Dutchbat soldiers saw that. ... There was a sort of fence on the left-hand side of the road to Potocari. I heard then a young woman screaming very close by (4 or 5 meters away). I then heard another woman beg: "Leave her, she is only nine years old." The screaming suddenly stopped. I was so in shock that I could scarcely move. ... The rumour later quickly circulated that a nine year old girl had been raped.

That night, a DutchBat medical orderly came across two Serb soldiers raping a young woman:

"[W]e saw two Serb soldiers, one of them was standing guard and the other one was lying on the girl, with his pants off. And we saw a girl lying on the ground, on some kind of mattress. There was blood on the mattress, even she was covered with blood. She had bruises on her legs. There was even blood coming down her legs. She was in total shock. She went totally crazy."

Bosnian Muslim refugees nearby could see the rape, but could do nothing about it because of Serb soldiers standing nearby. Other people heard women screaming, or saw women being dragged away. Several individuals were so terrified that they committed suicide by hanging themselves. Throughout the night and early the next morning, stories about the rapes and killings spread through the crowd and the terror in the camp escalated.

Screams, gunshots and other frightening noises were audible throughout the night and no one could sleep. Soldiers were picking people out of the crowd and taking them away: some returned; others did not. Witness T recounted how three brothers – one merely a child and the others in their teens – were taken out in the night. When the boys' mother went looking for them, she found them with their throats slit.

Deportation of women

As a result of exhaustive UN negotiations with Serb troops, around 25,000 Srebrenica women were forcibly transferred to the Bosniak-controlled territory.

Some buses apparently never reached safety. According to a witness account given by Kadir Habibović, who hid himself on one of the first buses from the base in Potočari to Kladanj, he saw at least one vehicle full of Bosniak women being driven away from Bosnian government-held territory.

Column of Bosniak men

On the evening of 11 July 1995, word spread through the Bosniak community that able-bodied men should take to the woods, form a column together with members of the ARBiH's 28th Division and attempt a breakthrough towards Bosnian government-held territory in the north. The men believed they stood a better chance of surviving by trying to escape than if they let themselves fall into Serb hands.

Map of military operations during the Srebrenica massacre. Green arrow marks route of the Bosnian column

Around 10 pm on 11 July the Division command, together with the municipal authorities, took the decision, on their own initiative, to form a column and leave the safe area in an attempt to reach government-controlled territory around Tuzla.

The journey to Tuzla – a distance of 55 kilometres – entailed crossing extremely hilly terrain in the height of the summer heat. Most individuals started out with enough rations for only two days; by the third day, people were beginning to eat leaves and slugs. Dehydration made finding drinking water a major problem, along with lack of sleep and physical exhaustion – many were exhausted before setting out. There was little cohesion or sense of common purpose in the column.

Along the way, the column was shelled and ambushed. In severe mental distress, some of the refugees committed suicide. Others were induced to surrender. Survivors claimed they were attacked with a chemical agent that caused hallucinations, disorientation and strange behaviour. Infiltrators in civilian clothing confused, attacked and killed refugees, including the wounded. Many of those taken prisoner were killed on the spot. Others were collected together before being taken to remote locations for mass execution.

The attacks on the column broke it up into smaller segments. Only about one third of the men succeeded in crossing the asphalt road between Konjević Polje and Nova Kasaba. It was this group that eventually crossed Bosnian Serb lines to reach Bosnian government territory on and after 16 July. The vast majority of the victims of the massacre were members of the column who failed to complete the perilous journey.

Other groups

A second, smaller group of refugees (estimated at between 700 and 800) attempted to escape into Serbia via Mount Kvarac via Bratunac, or across the River Drina and via Bajina Bašta. It is not known how many were intercepted, arrested and killed on the way. A third group headed for Žepa, possibly having first tried to reach Tuzla. The estimates of the numbers involved vary widely, from 300 to around 850. In addition, small pockets of resistance apparently remained behind and engaged Serb forces.

Tuzla column departs

Almost all the 28th Division, 5500 to 6000 soldiers, not all armed, gathered in the village of Susnjari, in the hills north of the town of Srebrenica, along with about 7,000 civilians. They included a very small number of women, not more than ten. Others assembled in the nearby village of Jaglici.

At around midnight on 11 July 1995, the column started moving along the axis between Konjević Polje and Bratunac. The main column was preceded by a reconnaissance party of four scouts, approximately five kilometres ahead. Members of the column walked one behind the other, following the paper trail laid down by a de-mining unit.

The column was led by a group of 50–100 of the best soldiers from each brigade, carrying the best available equipment. Elements of the 284th Brigade were followed by the 280th Brigade, with them the Chief of Staff Ramiz Becirovic. Civilians accompanied by other soldiers followed and at the back was the independent battalion which was part of the 28th Division. The elite of the enclave, including the mother and sister of Naser Orić, accompanied the best troops at the front of the column. Others in the column included the political leaders of the enclave, medical staff of the local hospital and the families of prominent persons in Srebrenica. A small number of women, children and elderly travelled with the column in the woods. Each brigade was responsible for a group of refugees and many civilians joined the military units spontaneously as the journey got underway.

The column was between 12 and 15 kilometres long, about two and a half hours separating head from tail.

The breakout from the enclave and the attempt to reach Tuzla came as a surprise to the VRS and caused considerable confusion, as the VRS had expected the men to go to Potočari. Serb general Milan Gvero in a briefing referred to members of the column as "hardened and violent criminals who will stop at nothing to prevent being taken prisoner and to enable their escape into Bosnian territory.". The Drina Corps and the various brigades were ordered by the VRS Main Staff to assign all available manpower to the task of finding any Muslim groups observed, preventing them from crossing into Muslim territory, taking them prisoner and holding them in buildings that could be secured by small forces.

Ambush at Kamenica Hill

During the night, poor visibility, fear of mines and panic induced by artillery fire split the column in two.

On the afternoon of 12 July, the front section emerged from the woods and crossed the asphalt road from Konjevic Polje and Nova Kasaba. Around 18.00

hours, the RS Army located the main part of the column still in the hilly area around Kamenica (outside the village of Pobuđe). Around 20.00 hours this part of the column, led by the municipal authorities and the wounded, started descending Kamenica Hill (44°19'53"N 18°14'5"E) towards the road. After a few dozen men had crossed, soldiers of the RS Army arrived from the direction of Kravica in trucks and armoured vehicles including a white vehicle with UNPROFOR symbols, calling out for Bosniaks over the loudspeaker to surrender.

It was around this time that yellow smoke was observed, followed by observations of strange behaviour, including suicides, hallucinations and members of the column attacking one another. Numerous survivors interviewed by Human Rights Watch claimed they were attacked with a chemical agent that caused hallucinations and disorientation. Gen. Zdravko Tolimir was an advocate of the use of chemical weapons against the ArBiH.

Heavy shooting and shelling began, which continued into the night. The armed members of the column returned fire and all scattered. Survivors describe a group of at least 1000 engaged at close range by small arms. Hundreds appear to have been killed as they fled the open area and some were said to have killed themselves to escape capture.

RS Army and Ministry of Interior persuaded members of the column to surrender by promising them protection and safe transportation towards Tuzla under UNPROFOR and Red Cross supervision. Appropriated UN and Red Cross equipment was used to deceive the refugees into believing the promises. Surrendering prisoners' personal belongings were confiscated and some were executed on the spot.

The rear of the column lost contact with the front and panic broke out. Many people remained in the Kamenica Hill area for a number of days, unable to move on with the escape route blocked by Serb forces. Thousands of Bosniaks surrendered or were captured. Some prisoners were ordered to summon friends and family members from the woods. There were reports of Serb forces using megaphones to call on the marchers to surrender, telling them that they would be exchanged for Serb soldiers held captive by Bosniak forces. It was at Kamenica that VRS personnel in civilian dress were reported to have infiltrated the column.

Men from the rear of the column who survived this ordeal described it as a manhunt.

Sandići massacre

Exhumations in Srebrenica, 1996

Close to Sandići, on the main road from Bratunac to Konjević Polje, one witness describes the Serbs forcing a Bosniak man to call other Bosniaks down from the mountains. Some 200 to 300 men, including the witness' brother, followed his instructions and descended to meet the VRS, presumably expecting some exchange of prisoners would take place. The witness hid behind a tree to see what would happen next. He watched as the men were lined up in seven ranks, each some forty metres in length, with their hands behind their heads; they were then mowed down by machine gun fire.

The VRS also sent one of the civilians who wished to surrender back towards the column: one of his eyes had been gouged out, his ears had been cut off and a cross carved into his forehead.

A small number of women, children and elderly people who had been part of the column were allowed to join the buses evacuating the women and children out of Potočari. Among them was Alma Delimustafić, a soldier of the 28th Brigade; at this time, Delimustafić was in her civilian clothes and was released.

Trek to Mount Udrc

The central section of the column managed to escape the shooting and reached Kamenica at about 11.00 hours and waited there for the wounded. Captain Ejub Golić and the Independent Battalion turned back towards Hajdučko Groblje to help the casualties. A number of survivors from the rear, who managed to escape crossed the asphalt roads to the north or the west of the area, had joined those in the central section of the column. The front third of the column, which had already left Kamenica Hill by the time the ambush occurred, headed for Mount Udrc (44°16′59″N 19°3′6″E); crossing the main asphalt road, they then forded the river Jadar. They reached the base of the mountain early on the morning of Thursday, 13 July and regrouped. At first, it was decided to send 300 ARBiH soldiers back in an attempt to break through the blockades. When reports came in that the central section of the column had nevertheless succeeded in crossing the road at Konjević Polje, this plan was abandoned. Approximately 1,000 additional men managed to reach Udrc that night.

Snagovo ambush

From Udrc the marchers moved toward the River Drinjaka and on to Mount Velja Glava, continuing through the night. Finding a Serb presence at Mount Velja Glava, where they arrived on Friday, 14 July the column was forced to skirt the mountain and wait on its slopes before it was able to move on toward Liplje and Marcici. Arriving at Marcici in the evening of 14 July the marchers were again ambushed near Snagovo by Serb forces equipped with anti-aircraft guns, artillery and tanks.

According to Lieutenant Džemail Bećirović, the column managed to break through the ambush and, in so doing, captured a VRS officer, Major Zoran Janković—providing the Army of Bosnia and Herzegovina with a significant bargaining counter. This prompted an attempt at negotiating a cessation in the fighting, but negotiations with local Serb forces failed. Nevertheless, the act of repulsing the ambush had a positive effect on morale of the marchers, who also captured an amount of weapons and supplies.

Approaching the frontline

The evening of 15 July saw the first radio contact between the 2nd Corps and the 28th Division, established using a walkie-talkie captured from the VRS. After initial distrust on the part of the 28th Division, the brothers Šabić were able to identify each other as they stood on either side of the VRS lines. Early in the morning, the column crossed the asphalt road linking Zvornik with Caparde and headed in the direction of Planinci, leaving a unit of some 100 to 200 armed marchers behind to wait for stragglers.

The column reached Krizevici later that day, and remained there while an attempt was made to negotiate with local Serb forces for safe passage through the Serb lines into Bosnian government controlled territory. The members of the column were advised to stay where they were, and to allow the Serb forces time to arrange for safe passage. It soon became apparent, though, that the small Serb force deployed in the area was only trying to gain time to organise a further attack on the marchers. In the area of Marcici-Crni the RS armed forces deployed 500 soldiers and policemen in order to stop the split part of the column (about 2,500 people), which was moving from Glodi towards Marcici.

At this point, the column's leaders decided to form several small groups of between 100 and 200 persons and send these to reconnoiter the way ahead. Early in the afternoon, the 2nd Corps and the 28th Division of the ARBiH met each other in the village of Potocani. The presidium of Srebrenica were the first to reach Bosnian terrain.

Breakthrough at Baljkovica

The hillside at Baljkovica (44°27'N 18°58'E) formed the last VRS line separating the column from Bosnian-held territory. The VRS cordon actually consisted of two lines, the first of which presented a front on the Tuzla side against the 2nd Corps and the other a front against the approaching 28th Division.

On the evening of 15 July a heavy hailstorm caused the Serb forces to take cover. The column's advance group took advantage of this to attack the Serb rear lines at Baljkovica. During the fighting, the main body of what remained of the column began to move from Krizevici. It reached the area of fighting at about 3 am on Sunday, 16 July.

At approximately 05.00 hours on 16 July, the 2nd Corps made its first attempt to break through the VRS cordon from the Bosnian side. The objective was to force a breakthrough close to the hamlets of Parlog and Resnik. They were joined by Naser Orić and a number of his men.

Around 8 am on the morning of 16 July parts of the 28th Division, with the 2nd Corps of the RBiH Army from Tuzla providing artillery support, attacked and breached RS Army lines. There was fierce fighting across the general area of Baljkovica.

Captured heavy arms including two Praga self-propelled anti-aircraft guns were fired at the Serb front line and the column finally succeeded in breaking through to Bosnian government controlled territory and linking up with BiH units at between 1 pm and 2 pm on 16 July.

Baljkovica corridor

Following radio negotiations between the 2nd Corps and the Zvornik Brigade, the Zvornik Brigade Command, which had lost three lines of trenches, agreed to open a corridor to allow "evacuation" of the column in return for the release of captured policemen and soldiers. The Baljkovica corridor was open from 14.00 to 17.00 hours.

After the corridor was closed between 17.00 and 18.00 hours the Zvornik Brigade Command reported that around 5000 civilians, with probably "a certain number of soldiers" with them had been let through, but "all those who passed were unarmed".

Arrival at Tuzla

Only a few journalists witnessed the arrival of the column in Bosnian-held territory, most attention was focused on the reception of the women and children at the airbase in Tuzla (44°27′31″N 18°43′31″E). The few press and television reports described the arrival of 'an army of ghosts': men clad in rags, totally exhausted and emaciated by hunger. Some had no more than underwear, some were walking on bleeding feet wrapped in rags or plastic, and some were being carried on makeshift stretchers. There were men walking hand in hand with children; many were still visibly frightened. Some were delirious and hallucinating as a result of the immense stress they had endured. One soldier had begun firing on men in his own unit as they arrived in Baljkovica and was killed to prevent further bloodshed; the medical station set up by the Army of Bosnia and Herzegovina in Međeđa handed out large quantities of tranquillisers.

The survivors felt bitterness towards the UN because it had not been able to protect the "Safe Area." Bitterness and resentment was also directed towards the 2nd Corps of the ARBiH and there were a number of incidents. In one, a member of the 28th Division opened fire at the Corps Commander, Sead Delić, who had resisted all calls from his officers for a military push to link up with fleeing soldiers and civilians; a military police bodyguard was killed, while another returned fire and killed the sniper. Tensions were so great that 2nd Corps staff officers removed their insignia in order to avoid recognition. According to the Deputy Corps Commander, the division had "turned against the 2nd Corps." This lack of confidence in the 2nd Corps was nothing new, however, as the 28th Division had felt abandoned already in Srebrenica.

By 4 August or thereabouts, the ArBiH determined that 3,175 members of the 28th Division had managed to get through to Tuzla. 2628 members of the Division, soldiers and officers, were considered certain to have been killed. The approximate number of individual members of the column killed was estimated at between 8300 and 9722.

After the closure of the corridor

Once the corridor had closed Serb forces recommenced hunting down parts of the column still in areas under their control. Around 2,000 refugees were reported to be hiding in the woods in the area of Pobudje.

On 17 July 1995, "searching the terrain", the RS Army captured a number of Bosniaks. Four children aged between 8 and 14 captured by the Bratunac Brigade were taken to the military barracks in Bratunac. When one of them described seeing a large number of ARBiH soldiers committing suicide and shooting at each other, Brigade Commander Blagojević suggested that the Drina Corps' press unit should record this testimony on video. The fate of the boys remain uncertain.

On 18 July, after a soldier was killed "trying to capture some persons during the search operation", the Zvornik Brigade Command issued an order to execute prisoners in its zone of responsibility in order to avoid any risks associated with their capture. The order was presumed to have remained effective until it was countermanded on 21 July.

Plan to execute the men of Srebrenica

Although Serb forces had long been blamed for the massacre, it was not until June 2004—following the Srebrenica commission's preliminary report—that Serb officials acknowledged that their security forces planned and carried out the mass killing. A Serb commission's final report on the 1995 Srebrenica massacre acknowledged that the mass murder of the men and boys was planned. The commission found that more than 7,800 were killed after it compiled thirty-four lists of victims.

A concerted effort was made to capture all Bosniak men of military age. In fact, those captured included many boys well below that age and elderly men several years above that age who remained in the enclave following the take-over of Srebrenica. These men and boys were targeted regardless of whether they chose to flee to Potočari or to join the Bosnian Muslim column. The operation to capture and detain the Bosnian Muslim men was well organised and comprehensive. The buses which transported the women and children were systematically searched for men.

Mass executions

Mass executions in the Srebrenica massacre

The vast amount of planning and high-level coordination invested in killing thousands of men in a few days is apparent from the scale and the methodical nature in which the executions were carried out. A concerted effort was made to capture all Bosniak men of military age. In fact, those captured included many boys well below that age and elderly men above it.

The Army of Republika Srpska took the largest number of prisoners on 13 July, along the Bratunac-Konjević Polje road. It remains impossible to cite a precise figure, but witness statements describe the assembly points such as the field at Sandići, the agricultural warehouses in Kravica, the school in Konjević Polje, the football field in Nova Kasaba, the village of Lolići and the village school of Luke. Several thousands of people were herded together in the field near Sandići and on the Nova Kasaba football pitch, where they were searched and put into smaller groups. In a video tape made by journalist Zoran Petrović, a Serb soldier states that at least 3,000 to 4,000 men had given themselves up on the road. By the late afternoon of 13 July, the total had risen to some 6,000 according to the intercepted radio communication; the following day, Major Franken of Dutchbat was given the same figure by Colonel Radislav Janković of the Serb army. Many of the prisoners had been seen in the locations described by passing convoys taking the women and children to Kladanj by bus, while various aerial photographs have since provided evidence to confirm this version of events.

One hour after the evacuation of the females from Potočari was completed, the Drina Corps staff diverted the buses to the areas in which the men were being held. Colonel Krsmanović, who on 12 July had arranged the buses for the evacuation, ordered the 700 men in Sandići to be collected, and the soldiers guarding them made them throw their possessions on a large heap and hand over anything of value. During the afternoon, the group in Sandići was visited by Mladić who told them that they would come to no harm, that they would be treated as prisoners of war, that they would be exchanged for other prisoners and that their families had been escorted to Tuzla in safety. Some of these men were placed on the transport to Bratunac and other locations, while some were marched on foot to the warehouses in Kravica. The men gathered on the soccer ground at Nova Kasaba were forced to hand over their personal belongings. They too received a personal visit from Mladić during the afternoon of 13 July; on this occasion, he announced that the Bosnian authorities in Tuzla did not want the men and that they were therefore to be taken to other locations. The men in Nova Kasaba were loaded onto buses and trucks and were taken to Bratunac or the other locations.

The Bosnian men who had been separated from the women, children and elderly in Potočari numbering approximately 1,000 were transported to Bratunac and subsequently joined by Bosnian men captured from the column. Almost without exception, the thousands of Bosnian prisoners captured, following the take-over of Srebrenica, were executed. Some were killed individually or in small groups by the soldiers who captured them and some were killed in the places where they were temporarily detained. Most, however, were killed in carefully orchestrated mass executions, commencing on 13 July 1995 in the region just north of Srebrenica.

The mass executions followed a well-established pattern. The men were first taken to empty schools or warehouses. After being detained there for some hours, they were loaded onto buses or trucks and taken to another site for execution. Usually, the execution fields were in isolated locations. The prisoners were unarmed and in many cases, steps had been taken to minimise resistance, such as blindfolding them, binding their wrists behind their backs with ligatures or removing their shoes. Once at the killing fields, the men were taken off the trucks in small groups, lined up and shot. Those who survived the initial round of shooting were individually shot with an extra round, though sometimes only after they had been left to suffer for a time.

The process of finding victim bodies in the Srebrenica region, often in mass graves, exhuming them and finally identifying them was relatively slow.

Morning of 13 July : Jadar River

A small-scale execution took place prior to midday at the Jadar River on 13 July. Seventeen men were transported by bus a short distance to a spot on the banks of the Jadar River. The men were then lined up and shot. One man, after being hit in the hip by a bullet, jumped into the river and managed to escape.

Afternoon of 13 July: Cerska Valley

The first large-scale mass executions began on the afternoon of 13 July 1995 in the valley of the River Cerska, to the west of Konjevic Polje. One witness, hidden among trees, saw two or three trucks, followed by an armoured vehicle and an earthmoving machine proceeding towards Cerska. After that, he heard gunshots for half an hour and then saw the armoured vehicle going in the opposite direction, but not the earthmoving machine. Other witnesses report seeing a pool of blood alongside the road to Cerska that day. Muhamed Durakovic, a UN translator, probably passed this execution site later that day. He reports seeing bodies tossed into a ditch alongside the road, with some men still alive.

Aerial photos and excavations later confirmed the presence of a mass grave near this location. Ammunition cartridges found at the scene reveal that the victims were lined up on one side of the road, whereupon their executioners shot from the other. The bodies—150 in number—were covered with earth where they lay. It could later be established that they had been killed by guns. All were men, between the ages of 14 and 50. All but three of the 150 were wearing civilian clothes. Many had their hands tied behind their backs. Nine could later be identified and were indeed on the list of missing persons from Srebrenica.

Late afternoon of 13 July: Kravica

Later that same afternoon, 13 July 1995 executions were also conducted in the largest of four warehouses (farm sheds) owned by the Agricultural Cooperative in Kravica. Between 1,000 and 1,500 men had been captured in fields near Sandići and detained in Sandići Meadow. They were brought to Kravica, either by bus or on foot, the distance being approximately one kilometer. A witness recalls seeing around 200 men, stripped to the waist and with their hands in the air, being forced to run in the direction of Kravica. An aerial photograph taken at 14:00 hours that afternoon shows two buses standing in front of the sheds.

At around 18:00 hours, when the men were all being held in the warehouse, VRS soldiers threw in hand grenades and shot with various weapons, including rocket propelled grenades. The mass murder in Kravica seemed unplanned and seems to have started spontaneously when one of the warehouse doors suddenly swung open, according to trial testimony.

Supposedly, there was more killing in and around Kravica and Sandići. Even before the murders in the warehouse, some 200 or 300 men were formed up in ranks near Sandići and then were executed en masse with concentrated machine guns. At Kravica, it seems that the local population had a hand in the killings. Some victims were mutilated and killed with knives. The bodies were taken to Bratunac or simply dumped in the river that runs alongside the road. One witness states that this all took place on 14 July. There were three survivors of the mass murder in the farm sheds at Kravica.

Armed guards shot at the men who tried to climb out the windows to escape the massacre. When the shooting stopped, the shed was full of bodies. Another survivor, who was only slightly wounded, reports:

I was not even able to touch the floor, the concrete floor of the warehouse.... After the shooting, I felt a strange kind of heat, warmth, which was coming from the blood that covered the concrete floor and I was stepping on the dead people who were lying around. But there were even men (just men) who were still alive, who were only wounded and as soon as I would step on him, I would hear him cry, moan, because I was trying to move as fast as I could. I could tell that people had been completely disembodied and I could feel bones of the people that had been hit by those bursts of bullets or shells, I could feel their ribs crushing. Then I would get up again and continue....

When this witness climbed out of a window, he was seen by a guard who shot at him. He then pretended to be dead and managed to escape the following morning. The other witness quoted above spent the night under a heap of bodies; the next morning, he watched as the soldiers examined the corpses for signs of life. The few survivors were forced to sing Serbian songs, and were then shot. Once the final victim had been killed, an excavator was driven in to shunt the bodies out of the shed; the asphalt outside was then hosed down with water. In September 1996, however, it was still possible to find the evidence.

Analyses of hair, blood and explosives residue collected at the Kravica Warehouse provide strong evidence of the killings. Experts determined the presence of bullet strikes, explosives residue, bullets and shell cases, as well as human blood, bones and tissue adhering to the walls and floors of the building. Forensic evidence presented by the ICTY Prosecutor established a link between the executions in Kravica and the 'primary' mass grave known as Glogova 2, in which the remains of 139 people were found. In the 'secondary' grave known as Zeleni Jadar 5 there were 145 bodies, a number of which were charred. Pieces of brick and window frame which were found in the Glogova 1 grave that was opened later also established a link with Kravica. Here, the remains of 191 victims were found.

13–14 July: Tišća

As the buses crowded with Bosnian women, children and elderly made their way from Potočari to Kladanj, they were stopped at Tišća village, searched, and the Bosnian men and boys found on board were removed from the bus. The evidence reveals a well-organised operation in Tišća.

From the checkpoint, an officer directed the soldier escorting the witness towards a nearby school where many other prisoners were being held. At the school, a soldier on a field telephone appeared to be transmitting and receiving orders. Sometime around midnight, the witness was loaded onto a truck with 22 other men with their hands tied behind their backs. At one point the truck stopped and a soldier on the scene said: "Not here. Take them up there, where they took people before." The truck reached another stopping point where the soldiers came around to the back of the truck and started shooting the prisoners. The survivor escaped by running away from the truck and hiding in a forest.

14 July: Grbavci and Orahovac

A large group of the prisoners who had been held overnight in Bratunac were bussed in a convoy of 30 vehicles to the Grbavci school in Orahovac early in the morning of 14 July 1995. When they got there, the school gym was already half-filled with prisoners who had been arriving since the early morning hours and within a few hours, the building was completely full. Survivors estimated that there were 2,000 to 2,500 men there, some of them very young and some quite elderly, although the ICTY Prosecution suggested this may have been an over-estimation and that the number of prisoners at this site was probably closer to 1,000. Some prisoners were taken outside and killed. At some point, a witness recalled, General Mladić arrived and told the men: "Well, your government does not want you and I have to take care of you."

After being held in the gym for several hours, the men were led out in small groups to the execution fields that afternoon. Each prisoner was blindfolded and given a drink of water as he left the gym. The prisoners were then taken in trucks to the execution fields less than one kilometre away. The men were lined up and shot in the back; those who survived the initial shooting were killed with an extra shot. Two adjacent meadows were used; once one was full of bodies, the executioners moved to the other. While the executions were in progress, the survivors said, earth-moving equipment was digging the graves. A witness who survived the shootings by pretending to be dead, reported that General Mladić drove up in a red car and watched some of the executions.

The forensic evidence supports crucial aspects of the survivors' testimony. Both aerial and satellite photos show that the ground in Orahovac was disturbed between 5 and 27 July 1995 and again between 7 and 27 September 1995. Two primary mass graves were uncovered in the area and were named Lazete 1 and Lazete 2 by investigators.

The Lazete 1 gravesite was exhumed by the ICTY Prosecution between 13 July and 3 August 2000. All of the 130 individuals uncovered, for whom sex could be determined, were male; 138 blindfolds were uncovered in the grave. Identification material for 23 persons, listed as missing following the fall of Srebrenica, was located during the exhumations at this site. The gravesite Lazete 2 was partly exhumed by a joint team from the Office of the Prosecutor and Physicians for Human Rights between August and September 1996 and completed in 2000. All of the 243 victims associated with Lazete 2 were male and the experts determined that the vast majority died of gunshot injuries. In addition, 147 blindfolds were located.

Forensic analysis of soil/pollen samples, blindfolds, ligatures, shell cases and aerial images of creation/disturbance dates, further revealed that bodies from the Lazete 1 and 2 graves were removed and reburied at secondary graves named Hodžići Road 3, 4 and 5. Aerial images show that these secondary gravesites were created between 7 September and 2 October 1995 and all of them were exhumed in 1998.

14–15 July: Petkovići

Delegates of the International Association of Genocide Scholars (IAGS) had examined an exhumed mass grave of victims of the July 1995 Srebrenica massacre, outside the village of Potocari, Bosnia and Herzegovina in July 2007.

On 14 and 15 July 1995, another large group of prisoners numbering some 1,500 to 2,000 were taken from Bratunac to the school in Petkovići. The conditions under which these men were held at the Petkovići school were even worse than those in Grabavci. It was hot, overcrowded and there was no food or water. In the absence of anything else, some prisoners chose to drink their own urine. Every now and then, soldiers would enter the room and physically abuse prisoners, or would call them outside. A few of the prisoners contemplated an escape attempt, but others said it would be better to stay since the International Red Cross would be sure to monitor the situation and they could not all be killed.

The men were called outside in small groups. They were ordered to strip to the waist and to remove their shoes, whereupon their hands were tied behind their backs. During the night of 14 July, the men were taken by truck to the dam at Petkovići. Those who arrived later could see immediately what was happening there. A large number of bodies were strewn on the ground, their hands tied behind their backs. Small groups of five to ten men were taken out of the trucks, lined up and shot. Some begged for water but their pleas were ignored. A survivor described his feelings of fear combined with thirst thus:

I was really sorry that I would die thirsty, and I was trying to hide amongst the people as long as I could, like everybody else. I just wanted to live for another second or two. And when it was my turn, I jumped out with what I believe were four other people. I could feel the gravel beneath my feet. It hurt.... I was walking with my head bent down and I wasn't feeling anything.... And then I thought that I would die very fast, that I would not suffer. And I just thought that my mother would never know where I had ended up. This is what I was thinking as I was getting out of the truck. [As the soldiers walked around to kill the survivors of the first round of shooting] I was still very thirsty. But I was sort of between life and death. I didn't know whether I wanted to live or to die anymore. I decided not to call out for them to shoot and kill me, but I was sort of praying to God that they'd come and kill me.

After the soldiers had left, two survivors helped each other to untie their hands, and then crawled over the heap of bodies towards the woods, where they intended to hide. As dawn arrived, they could see the execution site where bulldozers were collecting the bodies. On the way to the execution site, one of the survivors had peeked out from under his blindfold and had seen that Mladić was also on his way to the scene.

Aerial photos confirmed that the earth near the Petkovići dam had been disturbed, and that it was disturbed yet again some time between 7 and 27 September 1995. When the grave here was opened in April 1998, there seemed to be many bodies missing. Their removal had been accomplished with mechanical apparatus, causing considerable disturbance to the grave and its contents. At this time, the grave contained the remains of no more than 43 persons. Other bodies had been removed to a secondary grave, Liplje 2, prior to 2 October 1995. Here, the remains of at least 191 individuals were discovered.

14–16 July: Branjevo

On 14 July 1995 more prisoners from Bratunac were bussed northward to a school in the village of Pilica, north of Zvornik. As at other detention facilities, there was no food or water and several men died in the school gym from heat and dehydration. The men were held at the Pilica school for two nights. On 16 July 1995, following a now familiar pattern, the men were called out of the school and loaded onto buses with their hands tied behind their backs. They were then driven to the Branjevo Military Farm, where groups of 10 were lined up and shot.

Dražen Erdemović—who confessed killing at least 70 Bosniaks—was a member of the VRS 10th Sabotage Detachment (a Main Staff subordinate unit) and participated in the mass execution. Erdemović appeared as a prosecution witness and testified: "The men in front of us were ordered to turn their backs. When those men turned their backs to us, we shot at them. We were given orders to shoot."

On this point, one of the survivors recalls:

When they shot, I threw myself on the ground... one man fell on my head. I think that he was killed on the spot. I could feel the hot blood pouring over me.... I could hear one man crying for help. He was begging them to kill him. And they simply said "Let him suffer. We'll kill him later."

— Witness Q :

Erdemović said that all but one of the victims wore civilian clothes and that, except for one person who tried to escape, they offered no resistance before being shot. Sometimes the executioners were particularly cruel. When some of the soldiers recognised acquaintances from Srebrenica, they beat and humiliated them before killing them. Erdemovic had to persuade his fellow soldiers to stop using a machine gun for the killings; while it mortally wounded the prisoners it did not cause death immediately and prolonged their suffering. Between 1,000 and 1,200 men were killed in the course of that day at this execution site.

Aerial photographs, taken on 17 July 1995 of an area around the Branjevo Military Farm, show a large number of bodies lying in the field near the farm, as well as traces of the excavator that collected the bodies from the field.

Erdemović testified that, at around 15:00 hours on 16 July 1995 after he and his fellow soldiers from the 10th Sabotage Detachment had finished executing the prisoners at the Branjevo Military Farm, they were told that there was a group of 500 Bosnian prisoners from Srebrenica trying to break out of a nearby Dom Kultura club. Erdemović and the other members of his unit refused to carry out any more killings. They were then told to attend a meeting with a Lieutenant Colonel at a café in Pilica. Erdemović and his fellow-soldiers travelled to the café as requested and, as they waited, they could hear shots and grenades being detonated. The sounds lasted for approximately 15–20 minutes after which a soldier from Bratunac entered the café to inform those present that "everything was over".

There were no survivors to explain exactly what had happened in the Dom Kultura. The executions at the Dom Kultura were remarkable in that this was no remote spot but a location in the centre of town on the main road from Zvornik to Bijeljina. Over a year later, it was still possible to find physical evidence of this crime. As in Kravica, many traces of blood, hair and body tissue were found in the building, with cartridges and shells littered throughout the two storeys. It could also be established that explosives and machine guns had been used. Human remains and personal possessions were found under the stage, where blood had dripped down through the floorboards.

Two of the three survivors of the executions at the Branjevo Military Farm were arrested by local Bosnian Serb police on 25 July and sent to the prisoner of war compound at Batkovici. One had been a member of the group separated from the women in Potočari on 13 July. The prisoners who were taken to Batkovici survived the ordeal and were later able to testify before the Tribunal.

Čančari Road 12 was the site of the re-interment of at least 174 bodies, moved here from the mass grave at the Branjevo Military Farm. Only 43 were complete sets of remains, most of which established that death had taken place as the result of rifle fire. Of the 313 various body parts found, 145 displayed gunshot wounds of a severity likely to prove fatal.

14–17 July: Kozluk

The exact date of the executions at Kozluk is not known, although it can be narrowed down to the period of 14 to 17 July 1995. The most probable dates are 15 and 16 July, not least due to the geographic location of Kozluk, between Petkovići Dam and the Branjevo Military Farm. It therefore falls within the pattern of ever more northerly execution sites: Orahovac on 14 July, Petkovići Dam on 15 July, the Branjevo Military Farm and the Pilica Dom Kultura on 16 July. Another indication is that a Zvornik Brigade excavator spent eight hours in Kozluk on 16 July and a truck belonging to same brigade made two journeys between Orahovac and Kozluk that day. A bulldozer is known to have been active in Kozluk on 18 and 19 July.

Among Bosnian refugees in Germany, there were rumors of executions in Kozluk, during which the five hundred or so prisoners were forced to sing Serbian songs as they were being transported to the executions site. Although no survivors have since come forward, investigations in 1999 led to the discovery of a mass grave near Kozluk. This proved to be the actual location of an execution as well, and lay alongside the Drina accessible only by driving through the barracks occupied by the Drina Wolves, a regular police unit of Republika Srpska. The grave was not dug specifically for the purpose: it had previously been a quarry and a landfill site. Investigators found many shards of green glass which the nearby 'Vitinka' bottling plant had dumped there. This facilitated the process of establishing links with the secondary graves along Čančari Road.

The grave at Kozluk had been partly cleared some time prior to 27 September 1995 but no fewer than 340 bodies were found there nonetheless. In 237 cases, it was clear that they had died as the result of rifle fire: 83 by a single shot to the head, 76 by one shot through the torso region, 72 by multiple bullet wounds, five by wounds to the legs and one person by bullet wounds to the arm. The ages of the victims were between 8 and 85 years old. Some had been physically disabled, occasionally as the result of amputation. Many had clearly been tied and bound using strips of clothing or nylon thread.

Along the Čančari Road are twelve known mass graves, of which only two—Čančari Road 3 and 12—have been investigated in detail by 2001. Čančari Road 3 is known to have been a secondary grave linked to Kozluk, as shown by the glass fragments and labels from the Vitinka factory. The remains of 158 victims were found here, of which 35 bodies were still more or less intact and indicated that most had been killed by gunfire.

13–18 July: Bratunac-Konjević Polje road

On 13 July, near Konjević Polje, Serb soldiers summarily executed hundreds of Bosniaks, including women and children.

The men who were found attempting to escape by the Bratunac-Konjević Polje road were told that the Geneva Convention would be observed if they gave themselves up. In Bratunac, men were told that there were Serbian personnel standing by to escort them to Zagreb for an exchange of prisoners. The visible presence of UN uniforms and UN vehicles, stolen from Dutchbat, were intended to contribute to the feeling of reassurance. On 17 to 18 July, Serb soldiers captured about 150–200 Bosnians in the vicinity of Konjevic Polje and summarily executed about one-half of them.

18–19 July: Nezuk-Baljkovica frontline

After the closure of the corridor at Baljkovica, several groups of stragglers nevertheless attempted to escape into Bosnian territory. Most were captured by VRS troops in the Nezuk—Baljkovica area and killed on the spot. In the vicinity of Nezuk, about 20 small groups surrendered to Bosnian Serb military forces. After the men surrendered, Bosnian Serb soldiers ordered them to line up and summarily executed them.

On 19 July, for example, a group of approximately 11 men was killed at Nezuk itself by units of the 16th Krajina Brigade, then operating under the direct command of the Zvornik Brigade. Reports reveal that a further 13 men, all ARBiH soldiers, were killed at Nezuk on 19 July. The report of the march to Tuzla includes the account of an ARBiH soldier who witnessed several executions carried out by police that day. He survived because 30 ARBiH soldiers were needed for an exchange of prisoners following the ARBiH's capture of a VRS officer at Baljkovica. The soldier was himself exchanged late 1995; at that time, there were still 229 men from Srebrenica in the Batkovici prisoner of war camp, including two men who had been taken prisoner in 1994.

At the same time, RS Ministry of the Interior forces conducting a search of the terrain from Kamenica as far as Snagovo killed eight Bosniaks. Around 200 Muslims armed with automatic and hunting rifles were reported to be hiding near the old road near Snagovo. During the morning, about 50 Bosniaks attacked the Zvornik Brigade line in the area of Pandurica, attempting to break through to Bosnian government territory. The Zvornik Public Security Centre planned to surround and destroy these two groups the following day using all available forces.

20–22 July: Meces area

According to ICTY indictments of Radovan Karadžić and Ratko Mladić, on 20 to 21 July 1995 near the village of Meces, Bosnian Serb military personnel, using megaphones, urged Bosnian men who had fled Srebrenica to surrender and assured them that they would be safe. Approximately 350 men responded to these entreaties and surrendered. Serb soldiers then took approximately 150 of them, instructed them to dig their own graves and summarily executed them.

After the massacre

ICMP's Podrinje Identification Project (PIP) was formed to deal with the identification primarily of victims of 1995 Srebrenica massacre. PIP includes a facility for storing, processing, and handling exhumed remains. Much of the remains are only fragments or commingled body fragments since they were recovered from secondary mass graves. The photo depicts one section of the refrigerated mortuary.

During the days following the massacre, American spy planes overflew the area of Srebrenica, and took photos showing the ground in vast areas around the town had been removed, a sign of mass burials.

On 22 July, the commanding officer of the Zvornik Brigade, Lieutenant Colonel Vinko Pandurević, requested the Drina Corps to set up a committee to oversee the exchange of prisoners. He also asked for instructions where the prisoners of war his unit had already captured should be taken and to whom they should be handed over. Approximately 50 wounded captives were taken to the Bratunac hospital. Another group of prisoners was taken to the Batkovići camp (near Bijeljina), and these were mostly exchanged later. On 25 July, the Zvornik Brigade captured 25 more ARBiH soldiers who were taken directly to the camp at Batkovići, as were 34 ARBiH men captured the following day.

Zvornik Brigade reports up until 31 July continue to describe the search for refugees and the capture of small groups of Bosniaks.

A number of Bosniaks managed to cross over the River Drina into Serbia at Ljubovija and Bajina Bašta. 38 of them were returned to RS. Some were taken to the Batkovići camp, where they were exchanged. The fate of the majority has not been established. Some of those attempting to cross the Drina drowned.

By 17 July 201 Bosniak soldiers had arrived in Žepa, exhausted and many with light wounds. By 28 July another 500 had arrived in Žepa from Srebrenica.

After 19 July 1995, small Bosniak groups were hiding in the woods for days and months, trying to reach Tuzla. Numerous refugees found themselves cut off for some time in the area around Mount Udrc. They did not know what to do next or where to go; they managed to stay alive by eating snails, leaves and mushrooms. The atmosphere was one of tension, hunger and desperation. On or about 23 July, the Bosnian Serbs swept through this area too, and according to one survivor they killed many people as they did so.

Meanwhile, the VRS had commenced the process of clearing the bodies from around Srebrenica, Žepa, Kamenica and Snagovo. Work parties and municipal services were deployed to help. In Srebrenica, the refuse that had littered the streets since the departure of the people was collected and burnt, the town disinfected and deloused.

Wanderers

Many people in the part of the column which had not succeeded in passing Kamenica did not wish to give themselves up and decided to turn back towards Žepa. Others remained where they were, splitting up into smaller groups of no more than ten. Some wandered around for months, either alone or groups of two, four or six men. Few knew the way and so attempted to navigate by following overhead power cables. They often found corpses, by now in a state of decomposition. Sometimes one group met another group from Srebrenica who knew of a deserted Bosniak village in the region; they would then proceed there together.

Some of the Bosniak men decided to retrace their steps towards the Srebrenica region, since this was familiar territory and they knew where to find food. From here, they would once again set out towards Žepa or attempt to reach Tuzla. Some arrived in Tuzla after many months, having been wandering around the area between Srebrenica and Udrc with absolutely no sense of direction. A few hundred managed to reach Žepa just before the Serb military, paramilitary and police forces occupied the enclave on 25 July 1995. Once Žepa had succumbed to the Serb pressure, they had to move on once more, either trying to reach Tuzla or crossing the River Drina into Serbia.

To feed themselves, the men took potatoes and other vegetables from the fields around the Serbian villages at night. The local Serb population therefore began to mount patrols around their villages. The Bosniaks would generally sleep by day and wait for the cover of darkness before moving on. This continued for a long time. For example, the people of Milici, a village on the route to Tuzla, discovered the disappearance of livestock in November 1995 and formed an armed group in search of stragglers from the column.

There are many stories recalling the experiences of those who lost contact with the column, their wanderings and the horrors they saw. One involves three young men aged 17, 18 and 19, who on several occasions attempted to cross the main Konjević Polje to Nova Kasaba road but were unsuccessful in doing so each time. They eventually managed to reach Žepa only after the enclave had fallen as well. The group had set up camp in a couple of deserted Bosniak villages where they managed to hide out for several months without attracting attention. Sometimes the teenagers would escort groups of other refugees as far as the next obstacle, before eventually returning to their base. Finally, on 26 April 1996, a full six months after the signing of the Dayton Accord, they crossed the Drina into Serbia.

Zvornik 7

The most famous group of seven men wandered about in occupied territory for the entire winter. On 10 May 1996, after nine months on the run and over six months after the end of the war, they were discovered in a quarry by American IFOR soldiers. They immediately turned over to the patrol; they were searched and their weapons (two pistols and three hand grenades) were confiscated. The men said that they had been in hiding in the immediate vicinity of Srebrenica since the fall of the enclave. They did not look like soldiers and the Americans decided that this was a matter for the police. The operations officer of this American unit ordered that a Serb patrol should be escorted into the quarry whereupon the men would be handed over to the Serbs.

The prisoners said they were initially tortured after the transfer, but later were treated relatively well. In April 1997 the local court in Republika Srpska convicted the group, known as the Zvornik 7, for illegal possession of firearms and three of them for the murder of four Serbian woodsmen. When announcing the verdict the presenter of the TV of Republika Srpska described them as the group of Muslim terrorists from Srebrenica who last year massacred Serb civilians. The trial was widely condemned by the international community as "a flagrant miscarriage of justice" and the conviction was later quashed for 'procedural reasons' following pressure from the international community. In 1999, the three remaining defendants in the Zvornik 7 case were swapped for three Serbs serving 15 years each in a Bosnian prison.

Reburials in the secondary mass graves

From approximately 1 August 1995 to 1 November 1995, there was an organised effort to remove the bodies from primary mass gravesites and transport them to secondary and tertiary gravesites. In the International Criminal Tribunal for the former Yugoslavia court case "Prosecutor v. Blagojevic and Jokic", the trial chamber found that this reburial effort was an attempt to conceal evidence of the mass murders. The trial chamber found that the cover up operation was ordered by the VRS Main Staff and subsequently carried out by members of the Bratunac and Zvornik Brigades.

The cover-up operation has had a direct impact on the recovery and identification of the remains. The removal and reburial of the bodies have caused them to become dismembered and co-mingled, making it difficult for forensic investigators to positively identify the remains. For example, in one specific case, the remains of one person were found in two different locations, 30 km apart. In addition to the ligatures and blindfolds found at the mass graves, the effort to hide the bodies has been seen as evidence of the organised nature of the massacres and the non-combatant status of the victims, since had the victims died in normal combat operations, there would be no need to hide their remains.

Greek Volunteers controversy

Greek Volunteer Guard

According to Agence France Presse (AFP), a dozen Greek volunteers fought alongside the Serbs at Srebrenica. They were members of the Greek

Volunteer Guard (ЕЕΦ), or GVG, a contingent of Greek paramilitaries formed at the request of Ratko Mladić as an integral part of the Drina Corps. The Greek volunteers were motivated by the desire to support their "Orthodox brothers" in battle. They raised the Greek flag at Srebrenica after the fall of the town at Mladić's request, to honour "the brave Greeks fighting on our side." Radovan Karadžić subsequently decorated four of them.

In 2005, Greek deputy Andreas Andrianopoulos called for an investigation into the role of Greek volunteers in Srebrenica. The Greek Minister of Justice Anastasios Papaligouras commissioned an inquiry, which had still not reported as of July 2010.

In 2009, Stavros Vitalis announced that the volunteers were suing the writer Takis Michas for libel over allegations in his book Unholy Alliance, in which Michas described aspects of the Greek state's tacit support for the Serbs during the Bosnian War. Insisting that the volunteers had simply taken part in what he described as the "re-occupation" of the town, Vitalis acknowledged that he himself was present with senior Serb officers in "all operations" for Srebrenica's re-occupation by the Serbs. Michas notes that the volunteers were treated like heroes and at no point did Greek justice contact them to investigate their knowledge of potential crimes to assist the work of the International Criminal Tribunal for the former Yugoslavia at The Hague.

End of the war

After the Markale massacre on 28 August, NATO launched a bombing campaign in Bosnia and Herzegovina lasting from 30 August until 20

September. The Dayton Peace agreement of November 1995 effectively ended the war.

Post-war developments

1995: indictment of Radovan Karadžić and Ratko Mladić   Edit

On 16 November 1995 Radovan Karadžić, "President of the Republika Srpska" and Ratko Mladić, Commander of the VRS, were indicted by the International Criminal Tribunal for the Former Yugoslavia for their alleged direct responsibility for the war crimes committed in July 1995 against the Bosnian Muslim population of Srebrenica.

1999 UN Secretary-General's report

In 1999, UN Secretary-General Kofi Annan submitted his report on the Fall of Srebrenica. In it, he acknowledged that the international community as a whole had to accept its share of responsibility for its response to the ethnic cleansing campaign that culminated in the murder of some 7,000 unarmed civilians from the town designated by the Security Council as a "safe area."

2002 Dutch government report

The Srebrenica massacre led to long-running discussions in the Netherlands. In 1996, the Dutch government asked the Netherlands Institute for War Documentation to conduct research into the events before, during and after the fall of Srebrenica. The resulting report was published in 2002—Srebrenica: a 'safe' area.[176] It concluded that the Dutchbat mission was not well considered and well-nigh impossible. The NIOD report is cited often, however, the Institute for War and Peace Reporting labelled the report "controversial", as "the sheer abundance of information makes it possible for anyone to pluck from it whatever they need to make their point". One of the authors of the report claimed some of the sources were "unreliable", and were only used to support another author's argument.

As a result of the report, the Dutch government accepted partial political responsibility for the circumstances in which the massacre happened and the second cabinet of Wim Kok resigned in 2002.

2002 First Republika Srpska report

In September 2002, the Republika Srpska Office of Relations with the ICTY issued the "Report about Case Srebrenica". The document, authored by Darko Trifunović, was endorsed by many leading Bosnian Serb politicians. It concluded that 1,800 Bosnian Muslim soldiers died during fighting and a further 100 more died as a result of exhaustion. "The number of Muslim soldiers killed by Bosnian Serbs out of personal revenge or lack of knowledge of international law is probably about 100...It is important to uncover the names of the perpetrators in order to accurately and unequivocally establish whether or not these were isolated instances." The report also examined the mass graves, claiming that they were made for hygiene reasons, question the legitimacy of the missing person lists and undermine a key witness' mental health and military history. The International Crisis Group and the United Nations condemned the manipulation of their statements in this report.

2003: Srebrenica Genocide Memorial

Wall of names at the Srebrenica Genocide memorial

On 30 September 2003, former US President Bill Clinton officially opened the Srebrenica Genocide memorial to honour the victims of the genocide. The total cost of the project was around $5.8 million. "We must pay tribute to the innocent lives, many of them children who were snuffed out in what must be called genocidal madness", Clinton said.

2004: Second Republika Srpska report and official apology

In 2004, the international community's High Representative Paddy Ashdown had the Government of Republika Srpska form a committee to investigate the events. The committee released a report in October 2004 which acknowledged that at least 7,000 men and boys were killed by Bosnian Serb forces, citing a provisional figure of 7,800.

The findings of the committee remain generally disputed by Serb nationalists, who claim it was heavily pressured by the High Representative, given that an earlier RS government report which exonerated the Serbs was dismissed. Nevertheless, Dragan Čavić, the president of Republika Srpska, acknowledged in a televised address that Serb forces killed several thousand civilians in violation of the international law, and asserted that Srebrenica was a dark chapter in Serb history.

In the report, because of "limited time" and to "maximize resources", the commission "accepted the historical background and the facts stated in the second-instance judgment 'Prosecutor vs. Radislav Krstić', when the ICTY convicted the accused for 'assisting and supporting genocide' committed in Srebrenica".

On 10 November 2004, the government of Republika Srpska issued an official apology. The statement came after a government review of the Srebrenica committee's report. "The report makes it clear that enormous crimes were committed in the area of Srebrenica in July 1995. The Bosnian Serb

Government shares the pain of the families of the Srebrenica victims, is truly sorry and apologises for the tragedy." the Bosnian Serb government said.

2005 Release of Scorpions massacre video

On 2 June 2005, video evidence was introduced at the Slobodan Milošević trial to testify to the involvement of members of police units from Serbia in the Srebrenica massacre.[189] The video, the only undestroyed copy of twenty and previously available for rental in the Serbian town of Sid, was obtained and submitted to the ICTY by Nataša Kandić, director of the Belgrade-based Humanitarian Law Center.

The video footage (starting about 2hr 35 min. into the proceedings) shows an Orthodox priest blessing several members of a Serbian unit known as the "Scorpions." Later these soldiers are shown visibly abusing civilians physically. They were later identified as four minors as young as 16 and two men in their early twenties. The footage then shows the execution of four of the civilians and shows them lying dead in the field. At this point the cameraman expresses disappointment that the camera's battery is almost out. The soldiers then ordered the two remaining captives to take the four dead bodies into a nearby barn, where they were also killed upon completing this task.

The video caused public outrage in Serbia. In the days following its showing, the Serbian government arrested some of the former soldiers identified on the video. The event was extensively covered by the newspaper Danas and radio and television station B92. Nura Alispahić, mother of the 16-year-old Azmir Alispahić, saw the execution of her son on television. She said that she was already aware of her son's death and said she had been told that his body was burned following the execution; his remains were among those buried in Potočari in 2003.

The executions took place on 16/17 July, in Trnovo, about 30 minutes from the Scorpions' base near Sarajevo.

On 10 April 2007, a special war crimes court in Belgrade convicted four former members of the Scorpions of war crimes, treating the killings as an isolated war crime unrelated to the Srebrenica genocide and ignoring the allegations that the Scorpions were acting under the authority of the Serbian Interior Ministry, MUP.

2005 U.S. Congress and other resolutions

On 27 June 2005, the United States House of Representatives passed a resolution (H. Res. 199 sponsored by Congressman Christopher Smith and Congressman Benjamin Cardin) commemorating the 10th anniversary of the Srebrenica genocide. The resolution was passed by an overwhelming majority of 370 to 1, the only one to vote no being Ron Paul, with 62 absent. The resolution states that:

...the policies of aggression and ethnic cleansing as implemented by Serb forces in Bosnia and Herzegovina from 1992 to 1995 with the direct support of Serbian regime of Slobodan Milošević and its followers ultimately led to the displacement of more than 2,000,000 people, an estimated 200,000 killed, tens of thousands raped or otherwise tortured and abused, and the innocent civilians of Sarajevo and other urban centres repeatedly subjected to shelling and sniper attacks; meet the terms defining the crime of genocide in Article 2 of the Convention on the Prevention and Punishment of the Crime of

Genocide, created in Paris on 9 December 1948, and entered into force on 12 January 1951.

State of Missouri Resolution: On 6 July 2005, State of Missouri passed the resolution recognising the Srebrenica Genocide.

City of St. Louis Proclamation: On 11 July 2005, City of St. Louis issued a Proclamation declaring 11 July Srebrenica Remembrance Day in St. Louis.

2005 Potočari Memorial bomb plot

On 6 July 2005, Bosnian Serb police found two powerful bombs at the memorial site just days ahead of a ceremony to mark the massacre's 10th anniversary, when 580 identified victims were to be buried during the ceremony and more than 50,000 people, including international politicians and diplomats, were expected to attend. The bombs would have caused widespread loss of life and injury had they exploded.

2005 UN Secretary-General's message to the 10th anniversary commemoration

In his address to the 10th anniversary commemoration at Potočari, the UN Secretary-General paid tribute to the victims of "a terrible crime – the worst on European soil since the Second World War", on a date "marked as a grim reminder of man's inhumanity to man". He said that the first duty of the international community was to uncover and confront the full truth about what happened, a hard truth for those who serve the United Nations, because great nations failed to respond adequately. There should have been stronger military forces in place, and a stronger will to use them.

Blame lay first and foremost with those who planned and carried out the massacre, assisted them, or harboured and continue to harbour them. However the UN also bore its share of responsibility, having made serious errors of judgement, rooted in a philosophy of impartiality and non-violence which, however admirable, was unsuited to the conflict in Bosnia; because of that the tragedy of Srebrenica would haunt the UN's history forever.

Rebuilding trust among the peoples of the region could only done by persisting in the struggle for justice, without which there could be no reconciliation, and no peace for the families of the victims, or for society as a whole.

The quest for justice remained incomplete while those charged with being the main architects of this massacre – Ratko Mladić and Radovan Karadžić – were still at large and had not been made to answer the charges against them before the International Criminal Tribunal. He called on all Bosnians to search for truth and reconciliation.

Even while addressing the crimes of the past, the most important obligation was to prevent such systematic slaughter ever recurring anywhere again. The world had to equip itself to act collectively against genocide, ethnic cleansing and crimes against humanity. The "responsibility to protect" had to be given tangible meaning, not just rhetorical support.

He committed the UN helping the people of Bosnia and Herzegovina to rebuild a viable economy and secure a peaceful, prosperous future among the family of nations.

2005 Perpetrators named

On 4 October 2005, the Special Bosnian Serb Government Working Group said that 25,083 people were involved in the massacre, including 19,473 members of various Bosnian Serb armed forces that actively gave orders or directly took part in the massacre. They have identified 17,074 by name.[201] It has also been reported that some 892 of those suspects still hold positions at or are employed by the government of Republika Srpska. The names are still held secret.

Exhumed Grave of Victims 2007.

By 2006, 42 mass graves have been uncovered around Srebrenica and the specialists believe there are 22 more mass graves. The victims identified number 2,070 while body parts in more than 7,000 bags still await identification. On 11 August 2006 over 1,000 body parts were exhumed from one of Srebrenica mass graves located in Kamenica.

2006 Suppressed list of perpetrators in positions of authority published

On 24 August 2006, the Sarajevo daily newspaper Oslobodjenje started publishing a secret list of over 800 Bosnian Serbs who had participated in the Srebrenica massacre and were believed to be still in positions of power at government and municipal level. The names of the 892 individuals concerned were listed among 28,000 Bosnian Serbs reported to have taken part in the massacre by the official Republika Srpska report on Srebrenica. The list had been withheld from publication with the report by the chief prosecutor of the Bosnian War Crimes Chamber, Marinko Jurcevic.

2006 Dutch Srebrenica medal controversy

In December 2006, the Dutch government awarded the Dutch UN peacekeepers that served in Srebrenica an insignia because they believe they "deserved recognition for their behaviour in difficult circumstances", also noting the limited mandate and the ill-equipped nature of the mission. However, survivors and relatives of the victims condemned the move calling it a "humiliating decision" and responded with protest rallies in The Hague, Assen (where the ceremony took place) and Bosnia's capital Sarajevo.

2007 Arrest of Zdravko Tolimir

On 31 May 2007, former Bosnian Serb general Zdravko Tolimir was apprehended by police from Serbia and the Bosnian Serb republic, turned over to NATO forces at the Banja Luka airport where he was read the ICTY indictment and formally arrested. On 1 June 2007 NATO forces conveyed him to Rotterdam where he was turned over to the International Criminal Tribunal for the Former Yugoslavia (ICTY) in The Hague. As of July 2010, Tolimir was being tried by the ICTY on charges of genocide, conspiracy to commit genocide, extermination, persecution and forcible transfer. The indictment accuses Tolimir of participating in the "joint criminal enterprise to remove the Muslim population" from Srebrenica as well as the enclave of Zepa.

On 12 December 2012, Tolimir was convicted of genocide and sentenced to life imprisonment.

2008 Arrest of Radovan Karadžić

Radovan Karadžić, with similar charges as Zdravko Tolimir, was arrested in Belgrade on 21 July 2008 (after 13 years on the run) and brought before Belgrade's War Crimes Court. He was transferred to the ICTY on 30 July 2008. As of July 2010 Karadžić was being tried at the ICTY on 11 charges of genocide, war crimes and crimes against humanity.

2009 EU Parliament resolution

On 15 January 2009, the Parliament of the European Union voted with overwhelming majority of 556 votes in favour, 9 against and 22 abstentions on a resolution calling for the recognition of 11 July as a day for EU commemoration of the Srebrenica genocide. Bosnian Serb politicians rejected the resolution, stating that such a commemoration is unacceptable to the Republika Srpska.

2010 and 2012 Serbia's official apologies

In late March 2010, Serbian Parliament passed a resolution condemning the Srebrenica massacre and apologizing for Serbia not doing more to prevent the tragedy. The motion was passed by a narrow margin with 127 out of 250 MPs voting in favor, with 173 legislators present during the vote. The Socialist Party of Serbia, formerly under Slobodan Milošević and now under new leadership, voted in favor of adopting the resolution. Opposition parties, in turn, expressed their discontent with the resolution claiming its text was "shameful" for Serbia, either claiming the wording was too strong or too weak. Some relatives of Bosniak victims were also unhappy with the apology, as it did not use the word 'genocide', but rather pointed at the Bosnian Genocide case ruling of the International Court of Justice. Serbian president, Boris Tadić, said that the declaration is the highest expression of patriotism and that it represents distancing from crimes. Sulejman Tihić, former Bosniak member of the Presidency of Bosnia and Herzegovina and the current President of the House of Peoples of Bosnia and Herzegovina stated that now Bosnia and Herzegovina must adopt a similar resolution condemning crimes against Serbs and Croats.

On 25 April 2013, President Tomislav Nikolic apologised for the massacre: "I kneel and ask for forgiveness for Serbia for the crime committed in

Srebrenica. I apologise for the crimes committed by any individual in the name of our state and our people."]

2010 Second Republika Srpska report revision

On 21 April 2010, the government of Milorad Dodik, the prime minister of Republika Srpska, initiated a revision of the 2004 report saying that the numbers of killed were exaggerated and the report was manipulated by a former peace envoy. The Office of the High Representative responded by saying: "The Republika Srpska government should reconsider its conclusions and align itself with the facts and legal requirements and act accordingly, rather than inflicting emotional distress on the survivors, torture history and denigrate the public image of the country".

On 12 July 2010, at the 15th anniversary of the massacre, Milorad Dodik said that he acknowledged the killings that happened on the site, but did not regard what happened at Srebrenica as genocide.

2013 Supreme Court of the Netherlands judgement

In a judgement dated 6 September 2013, Supreme Court of the Netherlands, the Netherlands as a state was found responsible for the death of the three of the murdered men. The court also found that it was the government of the Netherlands which had the "effective control" over its troops. The rationale for finding that the Netherlands exercised "effective control" over Dutchbat was given as Art. 8 of the Articles on State Responsibility, which it defines as "factual control over specific conduct." The ruling also meant that relatives of these victims of the genocide are able to pursue the government of the Netherlands for compensation.

2015 Russia vetoes UN resolution

On July 8, 2015, Russia vetoed a United Nations Security Council resolution that would have condemned the Srebrenica massacre as a genocide. The resolution was intended to mark the 20th anniversary of the killing of 8,000 Muslim men and boys. China, Nigeria, Angola and Venezuela abstained and the remaining 10 members of the council voted in favour. Lobbied by the Republika Srpska and Serbia, the veto was praised by Serbian President Tomislav Nikolić stating that Russia had "prevented an attempt of smearing the entire Serbian nation as genocidal" and proven itself as a true and honest friend.

DNA analysis

Through the use of DNA profiling, the International Commission on Missing Persons (ICMP) has revealed the identity of 6,598 persons missing from the July 1995 fall of Srebrenica, by analysing DNA profiles extracted from bone samples of exhumed human remains and matching them to the DNA profiles obtained from blood samples donated by relatives of the missing. The overall high matching rate between DNA extracted from these bone and blood samples leads ICMP to support an estimate of close to 8,100 individuals missing from the fall of Srebrenica.

International Criminal Tribunal for the former Yugoslavia [ICTY]

Under Resolutions 808 and 827 (1993), the UN Security Council established the International Criminal Tribunal for the Former Yugoslavia (ICTY) to try those responsible for violations of international humanitarian law, including genocide, on the territory of the former Yugoslavia.

Two officers of the Army of the Republika Srpska have been convicted by the Tribunal for their involvement in the Srebrenica genocide, Radislav Krstić and Vidoje Blagojević. General Krstić, who led the assault on Srebrenica alongside Ratko Mladić, was convicted by the tribunal of aiding and abetting genocide and received a sentence of 35 years imprisonment. Colonel Blagojević received a sentence of 18 years imprisonment for crimes against humanity. Krstić was the first European to be convicted on a charge of genocide by an international tribunal since the Nuremberg trials and only the third person ever to have been convicted by an international tribunal under the 1948 Convention on the Prevention and Punishment of the Crime of Genocide. The ICTY's final ruling was that the Srebrenica massacre was indeed an act of genocide.

Slobodan Milošević was accused of genocide or complicity in genocide in territories within Bosnia and Herzegovina, including Srebrenica, but he died on 11 March 2006 during his ICTY trial and so no verdict was returned.

On 10 June 2010, seven senior Serb military and police officers, Vujadin Popović, Ljubiša Beara, Drago Nikolić, Ljubomir Borovčanin, Vinko Pandurević, Radivoje Miletić and Milan Gvero, were found guilty of various crimes ranging from genocide to murder and deportation. Popović and Beara were found guilty of genocide, extermination, murder, and persecution over the genocide, and were sentenced to life in prison. Nikolić was found guilty of aiding and abetting genocide, extermination, murder, and persecution and received 35 years in prison. Borovčanin was convicted of aiding and abetting extermination, murder, persecution, forcible transfer, murder as a crime against humanity and as a violation of the laws of customs of war, and was sentenced to 17 years in prison. Miletić was found guilty of murder by majority, persecution, and inhumane acts, specifically forcible transfer, and received 19 years in prison. Gvero was found guilty of persecution and inhumane acts and sentenced to five years in prison, but was acquitted of one count of murder and one count of deportation. Pandurević was found guilty of aiding and abetting murder, persecution and inhumane acts, but was acquitted of charges of genocide, extermination and deportation, and sentenced to 13 years in prison. On 10 September 2010, after the prosecution filed an appeal, Vujadin Popović, Ljubiša Beara, Drago Nikolić, Vinko Pandurević, Radivoje Miletić and Milan Gvero could face more charges or longer sentences.

In 2011, the former Chief of the General staff of the Yugoslav Army, Momčilo Perišić, was sentenced to 27 years in prison for aiding and abetting murder because he provided salaries, ammunition, staff and fuel to the VRS officers. The judges, however, ruled that Perišić did not have effective control over Mladić and other VRS officers involved in the crimes. According to the Trial Chamber, the evidence proved Perišić's inability to impose binding orders on Mladić.

On 31 May 2007, Zdravko Tolimir, a long time fugitive and a former general in the Army of the Republika Srpska indicted by the Prosecutor of the ICTY on genocide charges in the 1992–95 Bosnia war was arrested by Serbian and Bosnian police. Tolimir – "Chemical Zdravko" – is infamous for requesting the use of chemical weapons and proposing military strikes against refugees at Zepa. Ratko Mladić's deputy in charge of intelligence and security and a key commander at the time of Srebrenica, Tolimir is also believed to be one of the organisers of the support network protecting Mladić and helping him elude justice. Tolimir's trial began on 26 February 2010; he has chosen to represent himself.

Radovan Karadžić and Ratko Mladić have been indicted by the ICTY for genocide and complicity in genocide in several municipalities within Bosnia and Herzegovina, including Srebrenica. Karadžić was captured in Serbia on

21 July 2008 and Mladić, on 26 May 2011. Karadžić declined to enter a plea at his first appearance before the war crimes tribunal on 31 July 2008, a formal plea of "not guilty" was then made on his behalf by the judges. Karadžić insists on defending himself (as he is entitled to under the United Nations court's rules) while at the same time is setting up a team of legal advisers. Karadžić and Mladić, are both on trial on two counts of genocide and other war crimes committed in Srebrenica and also in other districts of Bosnia including Prijedor, Kljuc, Foča, Zvornik and other districts of Bosnia. Karadžić and Mladić are charged, separately, with:

Count 1: Genocide.

Municipalities: Bratunac, Foča, Ključ, Kotor Varoš, Prijedor, Sanski Most, Vlasenica and Zvornik.

To date this count has been dropped from the Prosecutor v. Karadzic trial. To quote the ICTY chamber upon this decision: "The evidence, even if taken at its highest, does not reach a level which a reasonable trier of fact could conclude that genocide occurred in the municipalities of Bosnia and Herzegovina".

Count 2: Genocide.

Municipality: Srebrenica.

Count 3: Persecutions on Political, Racial and Religious Grounds, a Crime Against Humanity.

Municipalities: Banja Luka, Bijeljina, Bosanska Krupa, Bosanski Novi, Bratunac, Brčko, Foča, Hadžići, Ilidža, Kalinovik, Ključ, Kotor Varoš, Novi Grad, Novo Sarajevo, Pale, Prijedor, Rogatica, Sanski Most, Sokolac, Trnovo, Vlasenica, Vogošća, Zvornik and Srebrenica.

Count 4: Extermination, a Crime Against Humanity.

Count 5: Murder, a Crime Against Humanity.

Count 6: Murder, a Violation of the Laws or Customs of War.

Count 7: Deportation, a Crime Against Humanity.

Count 8: Inhumane Acts (forcible transfer), a Crime Against Humanity.

Count 9: Acts of Violence the Primary Purpose of which is to Spread Terror among the Civilian Population, a Violation of the Laws or Customs of War.

Count 10: Unlawful Attacks on Civilians, a Violation of the Laws or Customs of War.

Count 11: Taking of Hostages, a Violation of the Laws or Customs of War.

International Court of Justice

In addition, the Srebrenica massacre was the core issue of the landmark court case, the Bosnian Genocide case at the International Court of Justice through which Bosnia and Herzegovina accused Serbia and Montenegro of genocide. The ICJ presented its judgment and cleared Serbia of direct involvement in genocide during the Bosnian war, but ruled that Belgrade did breach international law by failing to prevent the 1995 Srebrenica genocide, and for failing to try or transfer the persons accused of genocide to the ICTY, in order to comply with its obligations under Articles I and VI of the Genocide Convention, in particular in respect of General Ratko Mladić. Citing national security, Serbia obtained permission from the ICTY to keep parts of its military archives out of the public eye during its trial of Slobodan Milosevic, which may have decisively affected the ICJ's judgement in the lawsuit brought against Serbia by Bosnia-Herzegovina, as the archives were hence not on the ICTY's public record – although the ICJ could have, but did not, subpoena the documents themselves. Chief prosecutor's office, OTP, rejects allegations that there was a deal with Belgrade to conceal documents from the ICJ Bosnia genocide case.

National courts

Serbia

On 10 April 2007, a Serbian war crimes court sentenced four members of a paramilitary group known as the Scorpions to a total of 58 years in prison for the execution of six Bosniaks during the Srebrenica massacre of July 1995.

Bosnia and Herzegovina

On 11 June 2007, the ICTY transferred Milorad Trbic (former Chief of Security of the Zvornik Brigade of the Army of Republika Srpska) to Sarajevo to stand trial for genocide for his actions in and around Srebrenica before the War Crimes Chamber (Section I for War Crimes of the Criminal Division of the Court of Bosnia and Herzegovina; henceforth: the Court). Milorad Trbic – "[Is] charged with Genocide pursuant to Article 171 of the Criminal Code of Bosnia and Herzegovina (CC BiH). ... The trial commenced on 8 November 2007, and the Prosecutor is currently presenting his evidence."

The "Mitrović and others case ("Kravice")" was an important trial before the Court of Bosnia and Herzegovina. The accused "according to the indictment, in the period from 10 to 19 July 1995, as knowing participants in a joint criminal enterprise, the accused committed the criminal offence of genocide. This crime was allegedly committed as part of widespread and systematic attack against the Bosniak population inside the UN protected area of Srebrenica carried out by the Republika Srpska Army (RSA) and the RS Ministry of Interior, with a common plan to annihilate in part a group of Bosniak people." On 29 July 2008, after a two-year trial, the Court found seven men guilty of genocide for their role in the Srebrenica massacre including the deaths of 1000 Bosniak men in a single day. The court found that Bosniak men trying to escape from Srebrenica had been told they would be kept safe if they surrendered. Instead, they were transported to an agricultural co-operative in the village of Kravica, and later executed en masse.

On 20 April 2010, Croatia arrested Franc Kos, a member of the 10th commando detachment of the Army of the Republika Srpska, over genocide charges for the Srebrenica massacre. Bosnia and Herzegovina has an international warrant out for his arrest. He is currently awaiting trial.

On 29 April 2010, the United States extradited Marko Boškić on suspicions of having committed genocide. He later pleaded guilty.

On 18 January 2011, Israel arrested Aleksandar Cvetković, a veteran of the Bosnian Serb Army, after the Bosnian government filed an extradition request. Cvetković had moved to Israel in 2006 and secured citizenship through marriage to an Israeli. He was accused of having personally taken part in the executions of more than 800 men and boys, and initiated use of machine guns to speed up the killings. On 1 August 2011, a Jerusalem court approved Cvetković's extradition, and an appeal was denied in November 2012.

Božidar Kuvelja, a former Bosnian Serb policeman, was arrested in Čajniče, Bosnia and Herzegovina.

Guilty of genocide

Milenko Trifunović (commander of the 3rd "Skelani" Platoon, part of the 2nd Special Police Šekovići Squad) − found guilty, sentenced to 42 years.

Brano Džinić (special police force officer of the 2nd Special Police Šekovići Squad)[260] – found guilty, sentenced to 42 years.

Slobodan Jakovljević (special police force member of the 3rd "Skelani" Platoon)[260] – found guilty, sentenced to 40 years.

Branislav Medan (special police force member of the 3rd "Skelani" Platoon)[260] – found guilty, sentenced to 40 years.

Petar Mitrović (special police force member of the 3rd "Skelani" Platoon)[260] – found guilty, sentenced to 38 years.

Aleksandar Radovanović (special police force members of the 3rd "Skelani" Platoon)[260] – found guilty, sentenced to 42 years.

Milorad Trbić (assistant commander for Security with the Zvornik Brigade of the Republika Srpska Army) found guilty on one count of genocide and sentenced to 30 years in jail.

Radomir Vuković (special police force officer of the 2nd Special Police Šekovići Squad) – found guilty, sentenced to 31 years.

Zoran Tomić (special police force officer of the 2nd Special Police Šekovići Squad) – found guilty, sentenced to 31 years.

Marko Boškić (member of 10th Commando Squad of the Republika Srpska Army) – pleaded guilty, sentenced to 10 years.

Radovan Karadžić - found guilty, on 24 March 2016 he was sentenced to 40 years inprisonment.

Guilty of aiding and abetting genocide

Duško Jević (deputy commander of the interior ministry special police brigade and the commander of the Jahorina special police training center) – found guilty, sentenced to 35 years.

Mendeljev Đurić (commander of Jahorina special police training center's first company) – found guilty, sentenced to 30 years.

Guilty of crimes against humanity and war crimes

Stanko Kojić (member of the 10th Sabotage Unit of the Republika Srpska Army) – found guilty, sentenced to 43 years.

Franc Kos (commander of the First Platoon of the 10th Sabotage Unit of the Republika Srpska Army) – found guilty, sentenced to 40 years.

Zoran Goronja (member of the 10th Sabotage Unit of the Republika Srpska Army) – found guilty, sentenced to 40 years.

Vlastimir Golijan (member of the 10th Sabotage Unit of the Republika Srpska Army) – plead guilty, sentenced to 19 years.

Dragan Crnogorac (police officer) – found guilty, sentenced to 13 years.

Acquitted

Velibor Maksimović (special police force members of the 3rd "Skelani" Platoon) – acquitted.

Milovan Matić (member of the Republika Srpska Army)[260] – acquitted.

Teodor Pavelvić (member of the Republika Srpska Army) – acquitted.

Miladin Stevanović (special police force members of the 3rd "Skelani" Platoon) – acquitted.

Dragiša Živanović (special police force members of the 3rd "Skelani" Platoon) – acquitted.

Miloš Stupar (commander of the 2nd Special Police Šekovići Squad)[260] – found guilty, sentenced to 40 years, later acquitted.

Neđo Ikonić

Goran Marković

On trial

Božidar Kuvelja

Dejan Radojković

Indicted

Nedeljko Milidragović

Aleksa Golijanin

Awaiting extradition

Aleksandar Cvetković

Netherlands

Survivors and victims' relatives have sought to establish the responsibility of the State of the Netherlands and the United Nations for what happened at Srebrenica in civil law actions brought before The Hague District Court in the Netherlands.

In one case, 11 plaintiffs including the organisation "Mothers of the Enclaves of Srebrenica and Žepa", asked the court, to rule that the UN and the State of the Netherlands breached their obligation to prevent genocide, as laid down in the Genocide Convention and hold them jointly liable to pay compensation to the plaintiffs. On 10 July 2008, the court ruled that it had no jurisdiction against the UN; however, the court is set to rule against the State of the Netherlands. Plaintiffs have appealed the judgement in relation to UN immunity.

Another action was brought by a former UN interpreter Hasan Nuhanović and the family of Rizo Mustafić, an electrician employed by the UN at Srebrenica. They claimed that Dutch troops in the peacekeeping contingent responsible for security in the UN-protected zone allowed VRS troops to kill their relatives, Nuhanović's brother, father and mother and Mustafić. They argued that the Dutch Government had de facto operational command of the Dutch battalion in accordance with the Dutch Constitution (Article 97(2)), which grants the government superior command (oppergezag) over military forces. On 10 September 2008, the district court dismissed these claims and held that the State could not be held responsible because the Dutchbat peacekeepers were operating in Bosnia under a United Nations mandate and operational command and control over the troops had been transferred to the UN command.

On 5 July 2011, the court of appeal reversed the decision and held that the State was responsible for, and indeed actively coordinated, the evacuation once Srebrenica fell, and therefore is responsible for the decision to dismiss Nuhanović's brother and Mustafić from the Dutchbat compound. The court further held that this decision was wrong, because the Dutch soldiers should have known that they were in great danger of being tortured or killed. Both claimants are therefore eligible for compensation. On 6 September 2013, the Supreme Court dismissed the Government's appeal. The Dutch Government acknowledged the judgment.

On 16 July 2014, a Dutch court held the Netherlands liable for the killings of more than 300 Bosniaks at Srebrenica, although the same court ruled that the Netherlands was not liable for the other deaths in Srebrenica.

Analyses

Theodor Meron, the presiding judge of the ICTY Appeals Chamber, stated:

By seeking to eliminate a part of the Bosnian Muslims, the Bosnian Serb forces committed genocide. They targeted for extinction the 40,000 Bosnian Muslims living in Srebrenica, a group which was emblematic of the Bosnian Muslims in general. They stripped all the male Muslim prisoners, military and civilian, elderly and young, of their personal belongings and identification, and deliberately and methodically killed them solely on the basis of their identity.

In February 2007 the International Court of Justice (ICJ) concurred with the ICTY judgement, stating:

The Court concludes that the acts committed at Srebrenica falling within Article II (a) and (b) of the Convention were committed with the specific intent to destroy in part the group of the Muslims of Bosnia and Herzegovina as such; and accordingly that these were acts of genocide, committed by members of the VRS in and around Srebrenica from about 13 July 1995.

Role of Bosnian forces on the ground

In response to the suggestion that the Bosniak forces in Srebrenica made no adequate attempt to defend the town, the Report of the Secretary-General pursuant to General Assembly resolution 53/35—The Fall of Srebrenica, delivered to the 54th session of the United Nations General Assembly on 15 November 1999 states:

"Concerning the accusation that the Bosniaks did not do enough to defend Srebrenica, military experts consulted in connection with this report were largely in agreement that the Bosniaks could not have defended Srebrenica for long in the face of a concerted attack supported by armour and artillery."

"Many have accused the Bosniak forces of withdrawing from the enclave as the Serb forces advanced on the day of its fall. However, it must be remembered that on the eve of the final Serb assault the Dutchbat Commander urged the Bosniaks to withdraw from defensive positions south of Srebrenica town—the direction from which the Serbs were advancing. He did so because he believed that NATO aircraft would soon be launching widespread air strikes against the advancing Serbs." "A third accusation levelled at the Bosniak defenders of Srebrenica is that they provoked the Serb offensive by attacking out of that safe area. Even though this accusation is often repeated by international sources, there is no credible evidence to support it. Dutchbat personnel on the ground at the time assessed that the few "raids" the Bosniaks mounted out of Srebrenica were of little or no military significance. These raids were often organised in order to gather food, as the Serbs had refused access for humanitarian convoys into the enclave. Even Serb sources approached in the context of this report acknowledged that the Bosniak forces in Srebrenica posed no significant military threat to them. The biggest attack the Bosniaks launched out of Srebrenica during the more than two years during which it was designated a safe area appears to have been the raid on the village of Višnjica, on 26 June 1995, in which several houses were burned, up to four Serbs were killed and approximately 100 sheep were stolen. In contrast, the Serbs overran the enclave two weeks later, driving tens of thousands from their homes, and summarily executing thousands of men and boys. The Serbs repeatedly exaggerated the extent of the raids out of Srebrenica as a pretext for the prosecution of a central war aim: to create a geographically contiguous and ethnically pure territory along the Drina, while freeing their troops to fight in other parts of the country. The extent to which this pretext was accepted at face value by international actors and observers reflected the prism of "moral equivalency" through which the conflict in Bosnia was viewed by too many for too long."

Dispute regarding Serb casualties around Srebrenica

It is agreed by all sides that Serbs suffered a number of casualties during military forays led by Naser Orić. The controversy over the nature and number of the casualties came to a head in 2005, the 10th anniversary of the massacre. According to Human Rights Watch, the ultra-nationalist Serbian Radical Party "launched an aggressive campaign to prove that Muslims had committed crimes against thousands of Serbs in the area" which "was intended to diminish the significance of the July 1995 crime." A press briefing by the ICTY Office of the Prosecutor (OTP) dated 6 July 2005 noted that the number of Serb deaths in the region alleged by the Serbian authorities had increased from 1,400 to 3,500, a figure the OTP stated "[does] not reflect the reality." The briefing cited previous accounts:

The Republika Srpska's Commission for War Crimes gave the number of Serb victims in the municipalities of Bratunac, Srebrenica and Skelani as 995; 520 in Bratunac and 475 in Srebrenica.

The Chronicle of Our Graves by Milivoje Ivanišević, president of the Belgrade Centre for Investigating Crimes Committed against the Serbs, estimates the number of people killed at around 1,200.

For the Honourable Cross and Golden Freedom, a book published by the RS Ministry of Interior, referred to 641 Serb victims in the Bratunac-Srebrenica-Skelani region.

The accuracy of these numbers is challenged: the OTP noted that although Ivanišević's book estimated that around 1,200 Serbs were killed, personal details were only available for 624 victims. The validity of labeling some of the casualties as "victims" is also challenged: studies have found a significant majority of military casualties compared to civilian casualties. This is in line with the nature of the conflict—Serb casualties died in raids by Bosniak forces on outlying villages used as military outposts for attacks on Srebrenica (many of which had been ethnically cleansed of their Bosniak majority population in 1992). For example, the village of Kravica was attacked by Bosniak forces on Orthodox Christmas Day, 7 January 1993. Some Serb sources such as Ivanišević allege that the village's 353 inhabitants were "virtually completely destroyed". In fact, the VRS' own internal records state that 46 Serbs died in the Kravica attack: 35 soldiers and 11 civilians while the ICTY Prosecutor's Office's investigation of casualties on 7 and 8 January in Kravica and the surrounding villages found that 43 people were killed, of whom 13 were obviously civilians. Nevertheless, the event continues to be cited by Serb sources as the key example of crimes committed by Bosniak forces around Srebrenica. As for the destruction and casualties in the villages of Kravica, Siljkovići, Bjelovac, Fakovići and Sikirić, the judgement states that the prosecution failed to present convincing evidence that the Bosnian forces were responsible for them, because the Serb forces used artillery in the fighting in those villages. In the case of the village of Bjelovac, Serbs even used warplanes.

The most up-to-date analysis of Serb casualties in the region comes from the Sarajevo-based Research and Documentation Centre, a non-partisan institution with a multiethnic staff, whose data have been collected, processed, checked, compared and evaluated by international team of experts. The RDC's extensive review of casualty data found that Serb casualties in the Bratunac municipality amounted to 119 civilians and 424 soldiers. It also established that although the 383 Serb victims buried in the Bratunac military cemetery are presented as casualties of ARBiH units from Srebrenica, 139 (more than one third of the total) had fought and died elsewhere in Bosnia and Herzegovina.

Serb sources maintain that casualties and losses during the period prior to the creation of the safe area gave rise to Serb demands for revenge against the Bosniaks based in Srebrenica. The ARBiH raids are presented as a key motivating factor for the July 1995 genocide. This view is echoed by international sources including the 2002 report commissioned by the Dutch government on events leading to the fall of Srebrenica (the NIOD report).

The efforts to explain the Srebrenica massacre as motivated by revenge have been dismissed as bad faith attempts to justify the genocide. The ICTY Outreach Programme notes that the claim that Bosnian Serb forces killed the prisoners from Srebrenica in revenge for crimes committed by Bosnian Muslim forces against Serbs in the villages around Srebrenica provides no defence under international law and soldiers, certainly experienced officers, would be aware of the fact. To offer revenge as a justification for crimes is to attack the rule of law, and civilization itself, and nor does revenge provide moral justification for killing people simply because they share the same ethnicity as others who perpetrated crimes. The methodical planning and mobilization of the substantial resources involved required orders to be given at a high command level. The VRS had a plan to kill the Bosnian Muslim prisoners, as Dragan Obrenović confirmed.

The UN Secretary-General's report on the fall of Srebrenica said: "Even though this accusation is often repeated by international sources, there is no credible evidence to support it... The Serbs repeatedly exaggerated the extent of the raids out of Srebrenica as a pretext for the prosecution of a central war aim: to create a geographically contiguous and ethnically pure territory along the Drina."

Claim that the planning of mass executions in Srebrenica defies military logic

During Radislav Krstić's trial before the ICTY, the prosecution's military advisor, Richard Butler, pointed out that by carrying out a mass execution, the Serb Army deprived themselves of an extremely valuable bargaining counter. Butler suggested that they would have had far more to gain had they taken the men in Potočari as prisoners of war, under the supervision of the

International Red Cross (ICRC) and the UN troops still in the area. It might then have been possible to enter into some sort of exchange deal or they might have been able to force political concessions. Based on this reasoning, the ensuing mass murder defied military explanation.

Dutchbat

The Dutch Battalion "Dutchbat" was found guilty by the courts in the Netherlands of failing to protect some of the Bosniak refugees in the Safe Area Minister Voorhoeve of the Netherlands had ordered that "under no circumstances was Dutchbat allowed to cooperate in the separate treatment of men." A NATO battalion is expected to be able to exercise judgement when confronted with a conflict between rules of engagement and a specific order designed to protect refugees; moreover, it was the Netherlands and not the UN that had effective control of Dutchbat.

On 13 July, "Dutchbat" expelled[why?] five Bosniak refugees from the United Nations compound. Later proceedings in Dutch courts have established legal liability of The Netherlands for the deaths of those expelled.

In 2013 the Dutch Supreme Court held the Netherlands responsible for the death of 3 Bosnian men who were expelled from a compound held by Dutchbat, on 13 July 1995.

Claims of problems in the UNPROFOR chain of command above "Dutchbat"

Brigadier General, Hagrup Haukland was UNPROFOR's Commander of the sector in which the killings of the Srebrenica Massacre started on 11 July 1995. At this time he was on vacation. His subordinate, Colonel Charles Brantz phoned Haukland twice on 9 July 1995 to inform him about the crisis in

Srebrenica. Confusion within his staff has been attributed in part to his being slow to return to his place of work, not arriving at Tuzla headquarters until 14 July.

Other problems within Haukland's staff included lack of cooperation between "the Dutch and the Pakistanis", according to Harald Valved (UNPROFOR military advisor). The 2002 report Srebrenica: a 'safe' area said that "The cadres consisted of clans of Norwegian, Pakistani and Dutch military that were incapable of adequate mutual cooperation."

In 2005 an unnamed officer on Haukland's multinational staff at Tuzla in 1995, disputed the claim by Haukland and Chief of Defence Arne Solli that the attack on Srebrenica was a surprise. The officer said "We knew early that the Serbs were amassing their forces around Srebrenica. At the end of June, Haukland informed the headquarters at Sarajevo again and again in regards to this".

In 2006 it was reported that "Haukland regularly informed Chief of Defence Arne Sollie about the conditions within Haukland's sector. When Haukland departed Bosnia on his vacation to Norway, he travelled on the same airplane as the defence minister".

The 2002 report Srebrenica: a 'safe' area, did not assign any blame to Haukland for the massacre.

Claims and retraction by retired NATO SACLANT

In March 2010, John Sheehan, NATO's Supreme Allied Commander Atlantic from 1994 to 1997, told a US Senate hearing that the Dutch had "declared a peace dividend and made a conscious effort to socialise their military – that includes the unionisation of their militaries, it includes open homosexuality", claiming that gay soldiers could result in events like Srebrenica. He claimed that his opinion was shared by the leadership of the Dutch armed forces, mentioning the name "Hankman Berman", who Sheehan added, had told him that the presence of gay soldiers at Srebrenica had sapped morale and contributed to the disaster. General van den Breemen denied having said such a thing and called Sheehan's comments "total nonsense", Sheehan's remarks were also dismissed by the Dutch authorities as, "disgraceful" and "unworthy of anyone in the military". Sheehan apologised to Dutch military officials on 29 March 2010, withdrawing his comments and blaming instead "the rules of engagement...developed by a political system with conflicting priorities and an ambivalent understanding of how to use the military."

Criticism of the 1995 UN Special Representative for the former Yugoslavia

In 2005, Professor Arne Johan Vetlesen said "Thorvald Stoltenberg's co-responsibility in Srebrenica boils down to that he through three years as a top broker contributed to create a climate - diplomatic, politic and indirectly militarily - such that Mladic calculated correctly when he figured that he could do exactly what he wanted with Srebrenica's Muslim population".

Aftenposten said that Srebrenica: a 'safe' area in 2002, criticises Stoltenberg, and includes the quote "... The appointment of Stoltenberg as a [peace] broker was unfortunate."

Denial and scepticism

Sonja Biserko, president of the Helsinki Committee for Human Rights in Serbia, and Edina Bečirević, the Faculty of Criminalistics, Criminology and Security Studies of the University of Sarajevo have pointed to a culture of denial of the Srebrenica genocide in Serbian society, taking many forms and present in particular in political discourse, the media, the law and the educational system.

The scepticism ranges from challenging the judicial recognition of the killings as an act of genocide to the denial of a massacre having taken place. The finding of genocide by the ICJ and the ICTY, has been disputed on evidential and theoretical grounds. The number of the dead has been questioned as has the nature of their deaths. It has been alleged that considerably fewer than 8,000 were killed and/or that most of those killed died in battle rather than by execution. It has been claimed that the interpretation of "genocide" is refuted by the survival of the women and children.

Critics, such as Edward S. Herman in his book The Srebrenica Massacre and the British journalist Mick Hume, cite a discrepancy between a figure of over 8,000 victims and the number of bodies found and identified as casting doubt on the explanation of the events, despite the long delays in locating mass graves and identifying the bodies in them.

During the Bosnian war, Slobodan Milošević had effective control of most Serbian media. Since the end of the war, scepticism about Srebrenica continues to be widespread among Serbs.

In March 2005, Miloš Milovanović, a former commander of the Serb paramilitary unit Serbian Guard who represents the Serbian Democratic Party in the Srebrenica Municipal Assembly said that "the massacre is a lie; it is propaganda to paint a bad picture of the Serbian people. The Muslims are lying; they are manipulating the numbers; they are exaggerating what happened. Far more Serbs died at Srebrenica than Muslims."

Individuals and groups who have challenged or denied the events at Srebrenica as genocide

Milorad Dodik, president of Republika Srpska, has repeatedly insisted that massacre cannot be labeled as genocide.

Milorad Dodik, President of Republika Srpska, stated in an interview with the Belgrade newspaper Večernje Novosti in April 2010 that "we cannot and will never accept qualifying that event as a genocide". Dodik disowned the 2004 Republika Srpska report acknowledging the scale of the killing and apologising to the relatives of the victims, alleging that the report had been adopted because of pressure from the international community. Without substantiating the figure, he claimed that the number of victims was 3,500 rather than the 7,000 accepted by the report, alleging that 500 listed victims were alive and over 250 people buried in the Potocari memorial centre died elsewhere. In July 2010, on the 15th anniversary of the massacre, Dodik declared that he did not regard the killings at Srebrenica as genocide, and maintained that "If a genocide happened then it was committed against Serb people of this region where women, children and the elderly were killed en masse" (referring to eastern Bosnia). In December 2010, Dodik condemned the Peace Implementation Council, an international community of 55 countries, for referring to the Srebrenica massacre as genocide.

Tomislav Nikolić, President of Serbia, stated on 2 June 2012 that "there was no genocide in Srebrenica. In Srebrenica, grave war crimes were committed by some Serbs who should be found, prosecuted and punished. [...] It is very difficult to indict someone and prove before a court that an event qualifies as genocide."

La Nation, a bi-monthly Swiss newspaper, published a series of articles claiming that 2,000 soldiers were killed in the "pseudo-massacre" in Srebrenica. The Society for Threatened Peoples and Swiss Association Against Impunity filed a joint suit against La Nation for genocide denial. Swiss law prohibits genocide denial.

Phillip Corwin, former UN Civilian Affairs Coordinator in Bosnia, advisor and contributor to the work of the Srebrenica Research Group[344] said "What happened in Srebrenica was not a single large massacre of Muslims by Serbs, but rather a series of very bloody attacks and counterattacks over a three-year period."

Lewis MacKenzie, former commander of the United Nations Protection Force (UNPROFOR) in Bosnia, was continuing to challenge the description of genocide in 2009 on the grounds firstly that the number of men and boys killed had been exaggerated by a factor of 4 and secondly that transfer of the women and children by bus contradicted the notion of genocide – the women would have been killed first if there had been an intent to destroy the group. Writing in the Journal of Military and Strategic Studies (Vol. 12, Issue 1, Fall 2009), MacKenzie expressed his opinion without reference to the detailed arguments published by the ICTY Trial and Appeal Chambers in the Krstic case judgements published several years earlier and confirmed by the ICJ since.

The Srebrenica Research Group, a group led by Edward S. Herman and including two former UN officials,[348] claimed in their conclusions published in Srebrenica And the Politics of War Crimes (2005), "The contention that as many as 8,000 Muslims were killed has no basis in available evidence and is essentially a political construct".

The description of Srebrenica as a genocidal massacre has been disputed by Yehuda Bauer and the director of the Simon Wiesenthal Center office in Jerusalem, Efraim Zuroff .

Genocide scholar William Schabas in his 2009 book Genocide in International Law: The Crime of Crimes summarises the legal opinions regarding the status of the atrocities committed in Srebrenica and throughout the Bosnian war, deeming them ethnic cleansing and not genocide, stating that "Ethnic cleansing is also a warning sign of genocide to come. Genocide is the last resort of the frustrated ethnic cleanser."

Yehuda Bauer described Srebrenica as "an act of mass murder, not a genocide" and stated that he could see no evidence that Serb forces intended, in whole or in part, to exterminate the Bosniaks.

The director of the Simon Wiesenthal Center office in Israel, Efraim Zuroff, also disagrees that Serb forces had genocidal intent. He explained: "As far as I know, what happened [in Srebrenica] does not [fit] the description or the definition of genocide. I think the decision to call it genocide was made for political reasons. Obviously a tragedy occurred, innocent people lost their lives and their memory should be preserved." Zuroff also called attempts to equate Srebrenica to the Holocaust "horrible" and "absurd", saying: "I wish the Nazis moved aside Jewish women and children before their bloody rampage, instead of murdering them, but that, as we know, did not happen."

VERDICT :

Radovan Karadzic was eventually arrested in Belgrade on 21 July 2008 and brought before Belgrade's War Crimes Court a few days later. Extradited to the Netherlands, he is in the custody of the International Criminal Tribunal for the former Yugoslavia in the United Nations Detention Unit of Scheveningen, where he was charged with 11 counts of war crimes. He is sometimes referred to by the Western media as the "Butcher of Bosnia", a sobriquet also applied to former Army of Republika Srpska (VRS) General Ratko Mladić. On 24 March 2016, he was found guilty of genocide in Srebrenica, war crimes and crimes against humanity, 10 of the 11 eleven charges in total, and sentenced to 40 years' imprisonment.

Ratko Mladic's trial is still ongoing at this date of publication.

SOURCES OF REFERENCES

^ a b c Potocari Memorial Center Preliminary List of Missing Persons from Srebrenica '95 [1]

^ a b c UN Press Release SG/SM/9993UN, 11/07/2005 "Secretary-General Kofi Annan's message to the ceremony marking the tenth anniversary of the Srebrenica massacre in Potocari-Srebrenica". Retrieved 9 August 2010.

^ a b Institute for War and Peace Reporting, Tribunal Update: Briefly Noted (TU No 398, 18 March 2005) [2]

^ Paramilitaries Get 15 – 20 Years for Kosovo Crimes – [Balkan Inzqsight http://balkaninsight.com/en/main/news/20364/]

^ "Serbia: Mladic "Recruited" Infamous Scorpions". Institute for War and Peace Reporting. [3]

^ a b Williams, Daniel. "Srebrenica Video Vindicates Long Pursuit by Serb Activist". The Washington Post. Retrieved 26 May 2011.

^ "European Parliament resolution of 15 January 2009 on Srebrenica". European Parliament. Retrieved 10 August 2009.

^ "Office of the High Representative – "Decision Enacting the Law on the Center for the Srebrenica-Potocari Memorial and Cemetery for the Victims of the 1995 Genocide"". Office of the High Representative in Bosnia and Herzegovina. Archived from the original on 6 June 2011. Retrieved 10 August 2009.

^ "Youth Initiative for Human Rights in Serbia letter to the Serbian President to commemorate the Srebrenica genocide". Youth Initiative for Human Rights in Serbia. Archived from the original on 18 July 2011. Retrieved 10 August 2009.

^ "Mladic shadow hangs over Srebrenica trial". The Guardian (London). 21 August 2006. Retrieved 1 November 2008.

^ Goetze, Katharina (31 October 2008). "ICTY – Tribunal Update". Institute for War & Peace Reporting. Retrieved 1 November 2008.

^ Mike Corder (20 August 2006). "Srebrenica Genocide Trial to Restart". The Washington Post. Retrieved 26 October 2010.

^ "International Criminal Tribunal for the former Yugoslavia (ICTY)" (PDF). Retrieved 10 July 2015.

^ "The New York Times". 3 August 2001. Retrieved 10 July 2015.

^ "The International Court of Justice" (PDF). Retrieved 10 July 2015.

^ "ICTY: The Conflicts". The International Criminal Tribunal for the former Yugoslavia. Retrieved 5 August 2013.

^ Kirsten Nakjavani Bookmiller (2008). The United Nations. Infobase Publishing. Retrieved 4 August 2013., p. 81.

^ Christopher Paul; Colin P. Clarke; Beth Grill (2010). Victory Has a Thousand Fathers: Sources of Success in Counterinsurgency. Rand Corporation. Retrieved 4 August 2013., p. 25.

^ Simons, Marlise (31 May 2011). "Mladic Arrives in The Hague". The New York Times.

^ "ICTY – Kordic and Cerkez Judgement – 3. After the Conflict" (PDF). Retrieved 11 July 2012.

^ a b c SPIEGEL ONLINE, Hamburg, Germany (12 July 2005). "Dealing With Genocide: A Dutch Peacekeeper Remembers Srebrenica". SPIEGEL ONLINE.

^ ICTY, [4], Case No. IT-98-33, United Nations, 2 August 2001 "Archived copy" (PDF). Archived from the original (PDF) on 8 June 2006. Retrieved 8 June 2006. PDF (685 KB), "Findings of Fact", paragraphs 18 and 26 "Archived copy" (PDF). Archived from the original (PDF) on 24 August 2006. Retrieved 24 August 2006.

^ "UN Srebrenica immunity questioned". BBC. 18 June 2008. Retrieved 1 November 2008.

^ a b Comprehensive report of the proceedings, www.vandiepen.com

^ "Under The UN Flag; The International Community and the Srebrenica Genocide" by Hasan Nuhanović, pub. DES Sarajevo, 2007, ISBN 978-9958-728-87-7 [5][6]

^ "ICTY "Prosecutor v. Krstic"" (PDF). United Nations. 5 March 2007. Archived from the original (PDF) on 26 March 2009. Retrieved 11 July 2012.

^ ICJ (26 February 2007). "The Application of the Convention on the Prevention and Punishment of the Crime of Genocide (Bosnia and Herzegovina v. Serbia and Montenegro) [2007] Judgment, ICJ General List No. 91" (PDF). p. 108 § 297.

^ Prosecutor vs Krstic, ICTY Appeals Chamber Judgement, Case No. IT-98-33, 19 April 2004, Para. 33. Retrieved 21 March 2011

^ http://www.icty.org/x/cases/tolimir/acjug/en/150408_judgement.pdf

^ "Over 7,000 Srebrenica Victims have now been recovered". ICMP. 11 July 2012.

^ "Srebrenica's yearly burial of atrocity victims". Euronews. 11 July 2012.

^ "Serbian president apologises for Srebrenica 'crime'". BBC News. 25 April 2013.

^ a b "Judgement of the Supreme Court of the Netherlands, First Chamber, 12/03324 LZ/TT (English translation)" (PDF). 6 September 2013. Retrieved 17 July 2015.

^ "Netherlands Supreme Court hands down historic judgment over Srebrenica genocide". Amnesty Int. 27 Sep 2013. Retrieved 15 July 2015.

^ a b "Dutch state 'liable' for 300 Srebrenica deaths". BBC. 16 July 2014. Retrieved 17 July 2015.

^ BBC news website, "Dutch state 'responsible for three Srebrenica deaths'", 5 July 2011. (Retrieved 13 July 2015). http://www.bbc.co.uk/news/world-europe-14026218

^ Comiteau, Lauren. "Court Says the Dutch Are to Blame for Srebrenica Deaths", Time. 6 July 2011. (Retrieved 14 July 2015). http://content.time.com/time/world/article/0,8599,2081634,00.html

^ a b "Russia threatens veto on UN vote calling Srebrenica 'a crime of genocide'". the Guardian.

^ Bilefsky, Dan and Sengupta, Somini (8 July 2015). "Srebrenica Massacre, After 20 Years, Still Casts a Long Shadow in Bosnia". New York Times. Retrieved 17 July 2015.

^ "20 years after the Srebrenica genocide: Parliament says "never again"". European Parliament Portal. Retrieved 10 July 2015.

^ "Expressing the sense of the House of Representatives regarding Srebrenica.". www.congress.gov. Retrieved 10 July 2015.

^ a b "ICTY: The attack against the civilian population and related requirements". Archived from the original on 19 February 2009.

^ ICTY, Prosecutor vs. Krstic, Trial Chamber Judgement, para. 12

^ Bratunac Municipality Officials, "Truth about Bratunac (Istina o Bratuncu)". 1995 [7][dead link]

^ "IDC: Podrinje victim statistics". Archived from the original on 7 July 2007.

^ Bosnian Institute UK, the 26-page study: "Prelude to the Srebrenica Genocide – mass murder and ethnic cleansing of Bosniaks in the Srebrenica region during the first three months of the Bosnian War (April–June 1992)", 18 November 2010.

^ "Naser Oric Trial Judgement, ICTY" (PDF). Retrieved 26 May 2011.

^ ICTY, Prosecutor vs. Radislav Krstic Judgement; United Nations; para. No.13 http://web.archive.org/web/20060205104015/http://www.un.org:80/icty/krstic/TrialC1/judgement/. Archived from the original on 5 February 2006. Retrieved 8 June 2006. Missing or empty |title= (help)

^ ICTY, Prosecutor vs. Krstic; Trial Chamber Judgement; United Nations; para. 13–17.

^ New York Times, "Life in the Valley of Death" by Scott Anderson, 29 May 2014.   http://www.nytimes.com/interactive/2014/05/29/magazine/srebrenica-life-in-the-valley-of-death.html?_r=2&smid=tw-share

^   Tony   Birtley,   ABC   News   Archive   Footage,   March   1993. http://www.youtube.com/watch?v=Cz_dVScxOtg

^ Judgment in the Oric case, par.110. The International Criminal Tribunal at the Hague

^ a b c "Srebrenica - a 'safe' are" (PDF). NIOD. 2011. p. 9. Retrieved 21 July 2015.

^ "Srebrenica - a 'safe' are" (PDF). NIOD. 2011. p. 20. Retrieved 21 July 2015.

^ Security Council. "Resolution 819". United Nations. 16 April 1993. para. No.1 [8]

^ a b c d e f g h i j k l m ICTY, Prosecutor vs. Kristic, Judgement.

^ a b The United Nations' Report on The Fall of Srebrenica Archived 22 April 2008 at the Wayback Machine. (1999) [A/54/549]

^ Ramet (2006), p. 443

^ Secretary General. "The Fall of Srebrenica". United Nations. 15 November 1999.   (PDF) http://web.archive.org/web/20051005122450/http://www.un.org/News/ossg/srebrenica.pdf. Archived from the original (PDF) on 5 October 2005. Retrieved 30 October 2005. Missing or empty |title= (help) PDF (871 KB)

^ ICTY. "Prosecutor vs Krstic, Appeals Chamber Judgement". United Nations. 19 April 2004. (PDF) http://web.archive.org/web/20090326134340/http://www.un.org/icty/krstic/Appeal/judgement/krs-aj040419e.pdf. Archived from the original (PDF) on 26 March 2009. Retrieved 11 July 2012. Missing or empty |title= (help) PDF (700 KB)

^ BALKAN WATCH The Balkan Institute 10 July 1995 A Weekly Review of Current Events Volume 2.26 Week in Review 3–9 July 1995 [9]

^ Krstic Judgement – 6. 6–11 July 1995: The Take-Over of Srebrenica "Archived copy". Archived from the original on 8 May 2009. Retrieved 8 August 2009.

^ LeBor, Adam (1 October 2008). "Complicity with Evil": The United Nations in the Age of Modern Genocide. Yale University Press. p. 97. ISBN 0300135149.

^ "1,500 Bosnian Serb troops overran the enclave of Srebrenica". CNN. 11 July 1995. Retrieved 7 October 2012.

^ a b "Krstic Judgement – 6. 6–11 July 1995: The Take-Over of Srebrenica" (PDF). United Nations. 5 March 2007. Retrieved 26 May 2011.

^ a b c d e f g h i j k l m n "Krstic Judgement – (d) 13–14 July 1995: Tišca". United Nations. 5 March 2007. Archived from the original on 8 May 2009. Retrieved 26 May 2011.

^ "Dutch Court Rules Netherlands Responsible for Three Deaths in Srebrenica Massacre in Bosnia - The Daily Beast". The Daily Beast.

^ Daruvalla, Abi (21 April 2002). "Anatomy of a Massacre". Time. Retrieved 20 July 2006.

^ Bosnia's Accidental Genocide, Bosnian Institute in UK. 30 September 2006.

^ a b Marlise Simons (6 September 2013). "Dutch Peacekeepers Are Found Responsible for Deaths". The New York Times. Retrieved 7 September 2013.

Dutchbat soldiers knew that outside the compound men were being killed and abused, the court summary said, but the soldiers decided not to evacuate most refugees, including the three men, along with the battalion and instead sent them away on 13 July.

^ ICTY – Krstic verdict – (ii) 12–13 July: Crimes Committed in Potocari – http://web.archive.org/web/20080726164855/http://www.un.org/icty/krstic/Tri alC1/judgement/krs-tj010802e-1.htm. Archived from the original on 26 July 2008. Retrieved 19 July 2008. Missing or empty |title= (help)

^ ICTY – Krstic verdict – (ii) 12–13 July: Crimes Committed in Potocari – http://web.archive.org/web/20080726164855/http://www.un.org/icty/krstic/Tri alC1/judgement/krs-tj010802e-1.htm. Archived from the original on 26 July 2008. Retrieved 19 July 2008. Missing or empty |title= (help) – paragraph 45

^ Srebrenica Massacre Survivors Sue Netherlands, United Nations—By Udo Ludwig and Ansgar Mertin. Der Spiegel, 5 June 2007.

^ Refugees tell of women singled out for rape Archived 15 October 2009 at the Wayback Machine.. BookRags.com (18 July 1995). Retrieved 13 August 2010.

^ [10] by Mark Danner, The US and the Yugoslav Catastrophe, also see Snjezana Vukic, "Refugees Tell of Women Singled Out for Rape", The Independent (London), 18 July 1995.

^ "Separation of boys, Krstic ICTY Potocari". Icty.org. 26 July 2000. Retrieved 26 May 2011.

^ "Separation, Popovic ICTY". Icty.org. Retrieved 26 May 2011.

^ "Separation, Krstic ICTY". Icty.org. 11 July 1995. Retrieved 26 May 2011.

^ a b Graham Jones. Srebrenica: A Triumph of Evil, CNN 3 May 2006

^ Writ of summons (4 June 2007), page 107-108.

^ Writ of summons (4 June 2007), page 101.

^ Writ of summons (4 June 2007), page 104.

^ "Radislav Krstic Trial Chambers Judgement". Icty.org. 5 March 2007. Retrieved 26 May 2011.

^ Rohde, David; "Account of Women Taken", Columbia University; 2 October 1995 [11]

^ a b c "ICTY: Radislav Krstić verdict – The Column of Bosnian Muslim Men". Archived from the original on 5 January 2008.

^ Witness P-104 evidence to the Blagojevic trial, ICTY Case IT-06-60-T, Trial Chamber Judgment, 17 January 2005, Footnote 460, p. 52 [12]. Retrieved 9 April 2010.

^ a b c Enver Hadzihasanovic evidence to the Krstic trial, 6 April 2001, ICTY transcript p 9528 [13]. Retrieved 7 April 2010.

^ a b c Daily Mail, "Europe's worst genocide since Hitler: How Dutch peacekeepers looked on as Karadzic's men butchered 8,000 at Srebrenica", by David Jones, 23 July 2008 [14]. Retrieved 9 April 2010.

^ "081027ED".

^ a b c "061106ED".

http://commdocs.house.gov/committees/intlrel/hfa49268.000/hfa49268_0.htm Testimony of Diane Paul to US House of Representatives Committee on International relations Subcommittee on International Operations and Human Rights hearing on the Betrayal of Srebrenica, p. 39. Retrieved 24 July 2010.

^ a b "BBC News - Europe - Serbs accused of chemical attacks".

^ a b SENSE Tribunal report, 22 August 2006 Archived 8 October 2007 at the Wayback Machine.

^ Testimony of I.N., J.C., J.T., G.I., N.T., Human Rights Watch Report "The Fall of Srebrenica and the Failure of UN Peacekeeping", 15 October 1995 (12. Trek through Serbian-Controlled Territory) [15]. Retrieved 7 April 2010.

^ Witness PW-139 evidence to the Popovic et al trial, 6 November 2006, ICTY transcript pp3756-3757 [16]. Retrieved 24 July 2010.

^ Enver Hadzihasanovic evidence to the Krstic trial, 6 April 2001, ICTY transcript p 9528. [17]. Retrieved 7 April 2010.

^ Trial of Miladin Stevanović, Court of Bosnia & Herzegovina case X-KRŽ-05/24-2, page 18, 29 July 2008 (PDF) http://web.archive.org/web/20110724143755/http://www.sudbih.gov.ba/files/do cs/presude/2009/Miladin_Stevanovic_(Kravice)_-_1st_instance_verdict.pdf. Archived from the original (PDF) on 24 July 2011. Retrieved 7 April 2010. Missing or empty |title= (help). Retrieved 7 April 2010.

^ a b Mevludin Orić evidence to the Popovic et al trial, 31 August 2006, ICTY transcript pp 1083 & 1084 [18]. Retrieved 7 April 2010.

^ a b ["Netherlands Institute for War Documentation". http://193.173.80.81/srebrenica/]

^ Col. Trkulja evidence concerning Gen. Gvero Order 03/4-1629, 13 July 1995, to the Popovic et al. trial, 11 September 2007, ICTY transcript pp 15183 & 15185 [19]. Retrieved 7 April 2010.

^ Richard Butler evidence to the Blagojevic trial, 13 November 2003, ICTY transcript pp 4470–4471 [20]. Retrieved 7 April 2010.

^ a b c The Events in and Around Srebrenica between 10 and 19 July 1995" (The Republika Srpska Srebrenica Report 2004), June 2004, p 15 [21]. Retrieved 8 April 2010.

^ "Yugoslavia Has Long-Standing Poison Gas Program by Karel Knip, Rotterdam NRC Handelsblad 24 April 99 pp 1, 5. Retrieved 24 July 2010". Fas.org. Retrieved 26 May 2011.

^ a b Witness PW-139 evidence to the Popovic et al trial, 6 November 2006, ICTY transcript pp3665-3666 [22]. Retrieved 11 April 2010.

103

^ ABiH Tuzla. Tuzla (Intel Dept) to 2nd Corps, 25/07/95, (Tuzla no.) 11.6.-1-414/95 (2nd Corps no.) 06-712-24-30/95, Results of meeting with persons from Srebrenica. This report was signed by Sarajlic Osman.

^ ABiH Tuzla. ABiH 2nd Corps (unnumbered). Additional statement by Ramiz Becirovic, 16/04/98, based on an earlier statement of 11/08/95.

^ The Events in and Around Srebrenica between 10 and 19 July 1995" (The Republika Srpska Srebrenica Report 2004), June 2004, p 17 [23]. Retrieved 17 April 2010.

^ Zoran Jankovic evidence to the Popovic et al trial, 27 October 2008, ICTY transcript p 27369 [24]. Retrieved 13 April 2010.

^ The Events in and Around Srebrenica between 10 and 19 July 1995" (The Republika Srpska Srebrenica Report 2004), June 2004, p 21 [25]. Retrieved 8 April 2010.

^ "The Events In and Around Srebrenica between 10 and 19 July 1995" (The Republika Srpska Srebrenica Report 2004), June 2004, pp 21–22 . Retrieved 8 April 2010.

^ a b c d The Events in and Around Srebrenica between 10 and 19 July 1995" (The Republika Srpska Srebrenica Report 2004), June 2004, p 22 [26]. Retrieved 8 April 2010.

^ Enver Hadzihasanovic evidence to the Krstic trial, 6 April 2001, ICTY transcript p 9532 [27]. Retrieved 7 April 2010.

^ a b ICTY, Trial Chamber judgment in Case IT-02-60-T, Blagojevic & Jokic, 17 January 2005 para. 467, [28]. Retrieved 9 April 2010.

^ a b c d e f Krstic Judgement – 11.A Plan to Execute the Bosnian Muslim Men of Srebrenica http://web.archive.org/web/20080105091809/http://www.un.org:80/icty/krstic/TrialC1/judgement/krs-tj010802e-1.htm. Archived from the original on 5 January 2008. Retrieved 16 December 2007. Missing or empty |title= (help)

^ Jean-René Ruez evidence to the Blagojevic trial, 19 May 2003 ICTY transcript p 480 [29]. Retrieved 7 April 2010.

^ Krstic Judgement (a) The Morning of 13 July 1995: Jadar River Executions http://web.archive.org/web/20090508011123/http://www.un.org:80/icty/krstic/TrialC1/judgement/krs-tj010802e-1.htm. Archived from the original on 8 May 2009. Retrieved 8 August 2009. Missing or empty |title= (help)

^ Krstic Judgement (b)The Afternoon of 13 July 1995: Cerska Valley Executions http://web.archive.org/web/20090508011123/http://www.un.org:80/icty/krstic/TrialC1/judgement/krs-tj010802e-1.htm. Archived from the original on 8 May 2009. Retrieved 8 August 2009. Missing or empty |title= (help)

^ "Srebrenica – a 'safe' area – Part IV: The repercussion and the aftermath until the end of 1995". Archived from the original on 12 November 2008.

^ Krstic – Judgement (c)Late Afternoon of 13 July 1995: Kravica Warehouse http://web.archive.org/web/20090508011123/http://www.un.org:80/icty/krstic/TrialC1/judgement/krs-tj010802e-1.htm. Archived from the original on 8 May 2009. Retrieved 8 August 2009. Missing or empty |title= (help)

^ "Krstic Judgement – (d) 13–14 July 1995: Tišca". United Nations. 5 March 2007. Archived from the original on 8 May 2009. Retrieved 26 May 2011.

^ Krstic Judgement (e)14 July 1995: Grbavci School Detention Site and Orahovac Execution site http://web.archive.org/web/20090508011123/http://www.un.org:80/icty/krstic/TrialC1/judgement/krs-tj010802e-1.htm. Archived from the original on 8 May 2009. Retrieved 8 August 2009. Missing or empty |title= (help)

^ Krstic Judgement (f) 14–15 July 1995: Petkovci School Detention Site and Petkovci Dam Execution Site http://web.archive.org/web/20090508011123/http://www.un.org:80/icty/krstic/TrialC1/judgement/krs-tj010802e-1.htm. Archived from the original on 8 May 2009. Retrieved 8 August 2009. Missing or empty |title= (help)

^ ICTY, Prosecutor vs Krstic, Judgement Archived 17 May 2008 at the Wayback Machine., II, B, 5 (g) "14 – 16 July 1995: Pilica School Detention Site and Branjevo Military Farm Execution Site Archived 8 May 2009 at the Wayback Machine.", par. 233.

^ a b ICTY, Prosecutor vs Krstic, Judgement Archived 17 May 2008 at the Wayback Machine., II, B, 5 (g) "14 – 16 July 1995: Pilica School Detention Site and Branjevo Military Farm Execution Site Archived 8 May 2009 at the Wayback Machine.", par. 234.

^ ICTY, Prosecutor vs Krstic, Judgement Archived 17 May 2008 at the Wayback Machine., II, B, 5 (g) "14 – 16 July 1995: Pilica School Detention Site and Branjevo Military Farm Execution Site Archived 8 May 2009 at the Wayback Machine.", par. 235.

^ ICTY, Prosecutor vs Krstic, Judgement Archived 17 May 2008 at the Wayback Machine., II, B, 5 (g) "14 – 16 July 1995: Pilica School Detention Site and Branjevo Military Farm Execution Site Archived 8 May 2009 at the Wayback Machine.", par. 236.

^ ICTY, Prosecutor vs Krstic, Judgement Archived 17 May 2008 at the Wayback Machine., II, B, 5 (g) "14 – 16 July 1995: Pilica School Detention Site and Branjevo Military Farm Execution Site Archived 8 May 2009 at the Wayback Machine.", par. 237.

^ a b ICTY, Prosecutor vs Krstic, Judgement Archived 17 May 2008 at the Wayback Machine., II, B, 5 (h) "16 July 1995: Pilica Cultural Dom Archived 8 May 2009 at the Wayback Machine.", par. 244.

^ Jean-René Ruez evidence to the Blagojevic trial, 19 May 2003 ICTY transcript pp 535–536 [30]. Retrieved 7 April 2010.

^ ICTY, Prosecutor vs Krstic, Judgement Archived 17 May 2008 at the Wayback Machine., II, B, 5 (h) "16 July 1995: Pilica Cultural Dom Archived 8 May 2009 at the Wayback Machine.", par. 245.

^ Richard Butler evidence to the Krstic trial 19 July 2000 ICTY transcript p 5431 [31]. Retrieved 7 April 2010.

^ Witness PW-139 evidence to the Popovice et al., 7 November 2006, ICTY transcript p 3690 http://www.icty.org/x/cases/popovic/trans/en/061107ED.htm

^ ICTY, Prosecutor vs Krstic, Judgement Archived 17 May 2008 at the Wayback Machine., II, B, 5 (g) "14 – 16 July 1995: Pilica School Detention Site and Branjevo Military Farm Execution Site Archived 8 May 2009 at the Wayback Machine.", par. 238.

^ Dean Manning, Srebrenica Investigation: Summary of Forensic Evidence – Execution Points and Mass Graves[dead link], 16 May 2000, Annex A, 4 "ČANČARI ROAD 12 – (SECONDARY GRAVE)", pp. 18–21.

^ ICTY, Prosecutor vs Krstic, Judgement Archived 17 May 2008 at the Wayback Machine., II, B, 5 (i) "Kozluk Archived 8 May 2009 at the Wayback Machine.", par. 253.

^ ICTY, Prosecutor vs Krstic, Judgement Archived 17 May 2008 at the Wayback Machine., II, B, 5 (i) "Kozluk Archived 8 May 2009 at the Wayback Machine.", par. 252.

^ ICTY, Prosecutor vs Krstic, Judgement Archived 17 May 2008 at the Wayback Machine., II, B, 5 (i) "Kozluk Archived 8 May 2009 at the Wayback Machine.", par. 249.

^ a b Dean Manning, Srebrenica Investigation: Summary of Forensic Evidence – Execution Points and Mass Graves[dead link], 16 May 2000, Annex A, 11 "KOZLUK – (PRIMARY GRAVE)", pp. 42–44.

^ ICTY, Prosecutor vs Krstic, Judgement Archived 17 May 2008 at the Wayback Machine., II, B, 5 (i) "Kozluk Archived 8 May 2009 at the Wayback Machine.", par. 250.

^ Dean Manning, Srebrenica Investigation: Summary of Forensic Evidence – Execution Points and Mass Graves[dead link] 16 May 2000.

^ ICTY, Prosecutor vs Krstic, Judgement Archived 17 May 2008 at the Wayback Machine., II, B, 5 (i) "Kozluk Archived 8 May 2009 at the Wayback Machine.", par. 251.

^ Dean Manning, Srebrenica Investigation: Summary of Forensic Evidence – Execution Points and Mass Graves[dead link], 16 May 2000, p. 9.

^ a b c US Sen. Arlen Spector address to Senate marking Srebrenica Genocide 13th anniversary, Congressional Record (Senate), 11 July 2008, pp S6597-S6598 http://web.archive.org/web/20110725030226/http://www.baacbh.org/site/en/?action=news&ID=65. Archived from the original on 25 July 2011. Retrieved 13 April 2010. Missing or empty |title= (help). Retrieved 13 April 2010.

^ ICTY, Prosecutor vs Krstic, Judgement Archived 17 May 2008 at the Wayback Machine., II, A, 7 (b) "The Column of Bosnian Muslim Men Archived 5 January 2008 at the Wayback Machine.", par. 63.

^ ICTY, Prosecutor vs Krstic, Judgement Archived 17 May 2008 at the Wayback Machine., II, B, 5 (j) "Smaller Scale Executions following the Mass Executions Archived 8 May 2009 at the Wayback Machine.".

^ a b c The Events in and Around Srebrenica between 10 and 19 July 1995" (The Republika Srpska Srebrenica Report 2004), June 2004, p 23 [32]. Retrieved 8 April 2010.

^ The Events in and Around Srebrenica between 10 and 19 July 1995" (The Republika Srpska Srebrenica Report 2004), June 2004, pp 23–24 [33]. Retrieved 8 April 2010.

^ "paras 20.6 and 20.7". United Nations. 5 March 2007. Archived from the original on 29 August 2009. Retrieved 26 May 2011.

^ a b c d e f The Events in and Around Srebrenica between 10 and 19 July 1995" (The Republika Srpska Srebrenica Report 2004), June 2004, p 24 [34]. Retrieved 8 April 2010.

^ Esma Palic evidence to the Popovic et al trial, 6 February 2006, ICTY transcript p 6939 [35]. Retrieved 7 April 2010.

^ Preston V. McMurry III. "The Officer Who First Took Charge of the Zvornik Seven". Prestonm.com. Archived from the original on 15 July 2011. Retrieved 26 May 2011.

^ Medienhilfe Ex-Jugoslawien – Monitoring Report – Media trial of the Zvornik Seven Archived 6 October 2007 at the Wayback Machine.

^ UNHCR report - Archived 27 June 2009 at the Wayback Machine.

^ Office of the High Representative Press Office Release, "Zvornik 7 Verdict", 15 December 1998 http://web.archive.org/web/20130411231122/http://www.ohr.int/ohr-dept/presso/pressr/default.asp?content_id=4683. Archived from the original on 11 April 2013. Retrieved 13 April 2010. Missing or empty |title= (help). Retrieved 13 April 2010.

^ ICTY: Prosecutor v. Blagojevic and Jokic Trial Chamber Judgment Case No. IT-02-60 Section II G Prosecutor v. Blagojevic and Jokic Archived 5 January 2008 at the Wayback Machine.

^ ICTY: Prosecutor v. Blagojevic and Jokic Trial Chamber Judgment Case No. IT-02-60 paragraph 382 Prosecutor v. Blagojevic and Jokic Archived 10 March 2007 at the Wayback Machine.

^ ICTY: Prosecutor v. Blagojevic and Jokic Trial Chamber Judgment Case No. IT-02-60 paragraph 383 Prosecutor v. Blagojevic and Jokic Archived 10 March 2007 at the Wayback Machine.

^ a b Durnford, Laura "Bridges of Bone and Blood" Archived 6 February 2007 at the Wayback Machine.

^ The Scotsman "Finding the Bodies To Fill Bosnia's Graves" commentary by Adam Boys (ICMP) comment # 16. Adam Boys Commentary

^ Wood, Peter "Pollen Helps War Crimes Forensics"

^ AFP; "Greek Volunteers Fought Alongside Bosnian Serbs." OMRI Daily News Digest, 13 July 1995;. Retrieved 31 July 2010.

^ Grohmann, Karolos; "Greece starts probe into Srebrenica massacre"; Reuters, 27 June 2006 "Archived copy". Archived from the original on 4 January 2009. Retrieved 26 August 2008.

^ Michas 2002, p. 22.

^ Michas 2002, pp. 17–41.

^ Smith, Helena (5 January 2003). "Greece faces shame of role in Serb massacre". The Guardian (UK). Retrieved 20 April 2010.

^ Koknar, Ali M. (14 July 2003). "The Kontraktniki : Russian mercenaries at war in the Balkans". Bosnian Institute.

^ The BALKAN Human Rights Web Pages. Cm.greekhelsinki.gr (4 July 2005). Retrieved 13 August 2010.

^ The BALKAN Human Rights Web Pages. Cm.greekhelsinki.gr (10 July 2005). Retrieved 13 August 2010.

^ Smith, Helena (1 August 2005). "Helena Smith@Athens". The Guardian (UK). Retrieved 21 April 2010.

^ "Greece: Suit Against Journalist For Srebrenica Claims to Go Forward". Balkan Investigative Reporting Network. 21 June 2010. Archived from the original on 25 July 2010.

^ Congress of North American Bosniaks, Interview, 5 August 2009 [36]. Retrieved 8 April 2010.

^ "The Greek role in Bosnia's war". YouTube. 10 July 2010. Retrieved 26 May 2011.

^ a b Ods Home Page Archived 28 July 2011 at the Wayback Machine.. Daccess-dds-ny.un.org. Retrieved 13 August 2010.

^ a b The Secretary-General's Statements Archived 12 September 2009 at the Wayback Machine.. United Nations. Retrieved 13 August 2010.

^ Links to documents. United Nations.org (9 September 2002). Retrieved 13 August 2010.

^ J.C.H. Blom et al. (2002) Prologue NIOD Report: Srebrenica. Reconstruction, background, consequences and analyses of the fall of a Safe Area

^ Karen Meirik (9 November 2005). "Controversial Srebrenica Report Back on Table". Institute for War & Peace Reporting (UK). Retrieved 20 November 2013.

^ "Oxford Review, 17 Apr 2002". Google News. Retrieved 5 February 2013.

^ Parlementair Documentatie Centrum [Parliamentary Documentation Centre] of Leiden University, Parlementaire enquête Srebrenica (2002–2003) (in Dutch). Retrieved 17 February 2007.

^ BBC News (16 April 2002), Dutch Government quits over Srebrenica. Retrieved 17 February 2007.

^ Report about Case Srebrenica – Banja Luka, 2002

^ Imaginary Massacres?, Time, 11 September 2002

^ "Clinton unveils Bosnia memorial". BBC News. 20 September 2003. Retrieved 20 April 2010.

^ Wilkinson, Tracy (21 September 2003). "Clinton Helps Bosnians Mourn Their Men". Los Angeles Times.

^ Rachel Kerr (2007). Peace and Justice. Polity. Retrieved 5 August 2013., p. 192.

^ Tanja Topić (1 July 2004). "Otvaranje najmračnije stranice" (in Serbian). Vreme.

^ "The Events in and Around Srebrenica Between 10th and 19th July 1995" (PDF).

^ "Bosnian Serbs issue apology for massacre, AP, 11 November 2004". Bosnia.org.uk. 11 November 2004. Retrieved 26 May 2011.

^ a b [37][dead link]

^ a b c War Crimes Prosecution Watch, 30 April 2007 http://web.archive.org/web/20101218032335/http://www.publicinternationalla w.org:80/warcrimeswatch/archives/wcpw_vol02issue18.html. Archived from the original on 18 December 2010. Retrieved 6 April 2010. Missing or empty |title= (help). Retrieved 6 April 2010.

^ International Herald Tribune, Janine di Giovanni, June 2005. http://web.archive.org/web/20100821092440/http://www.janinedigiovanni.com :80/srebrenica-ten-years-on.html. Archived from the original on 21 August 2010. Retrieved 6 April 2010. Missing or empty |title= (help). Retrieved 6 April 2010.

^ "Heartbroken mom sees son shot on TV", by Samir Krilic (AP report) in Cape Argus, 4 June 2005. http://web.archive.org/web/20100530220546/http://www.iol.co.za:80/index.ph p?set_id=1. Archived from the original on 30 May 2010. Retrieved 6 April 2010. Missing or empty |title= (help). Retrieved 7 April 2010.

^ Belgrade District Court War Crimes Chamber, amended indictment against Aleksandar Medic in Case K.V. 6/2005, 1 October 2008 [38]. Retrieved 7 April 2010.

^ Crimes of War Project. "Serbian Court Convicts Four over Killings in Scorpions Tape", by Anthony Dworkin. http://web.archive.org/web/20100526184030/http://www.crimesofwar.org:80/n ews-srebrenica3.html. Archived from the original on 26 May 2010. Retrieved 6 April 2010. Missing or empty |title= (help). Retrieved 6 April 2010.

^ "Votes Database: Bill: H RES 199", The Washington Post (27 June 2005). Retrieved 1 August 2008.

^ "Read The Bill: H. Res. 199 109th". GovTrack.us. Retrieved 3 June 2011.

^ Association of the Srebrenica Genocide Survivors in Saint Louis, Missouri Resolution[dead link]

^ Association of the Srebrenica Genocide Survivors in St. Louis, City of St. Louis Proclamation[dead link]

^ "Bombs found at memorial for Srebrenica genocide". The Independent (UK). 6 July 2005. Archived from the original on 4 March 2010. Retrieved 26 May 2011.

^ Wood, Nicholas (6 July 2005). "2 bombs found near Srebrenica". The New York Times. Retrieved 26 May 2011.

^ Alic, Anes (5 October 2005). "25,000 participated in Srebrenica massacre" Archived 15 May 2007 at the Wayback Machine., ISN Security Watch. Retrieved 1 August 2008.

^ "Bosnia-Herzegovina:Srebrenica: Still Waiting for the Truth"[dead link] (AI Index: /003/2005), Amnesty International (1 April 2005). Retrieved 1 August 2008.

^ Weinberg, Bill (11 July 2006)."Srebrenica: 11 years later, still no justice" Archived 15 July 2006 at the Wayback Machine., World War 4 Report. Retrieved 1 August 2008.

^ Mass Grave Yields over 1,000 Body Parts, Reuters 11 August 2006 "Archived copy". Archived from the original on 15 January 2008. Retrieved 14 August 2006.

^ Avdić, Avdo (24 August 2006). "'Oslobođenje' objavljuje spisak za Srebrenicu", Oslobođenje. Retrieved 1 August 2008.

^ IWPR ICTY – Tribunal Update (26 August 2006) [39]. Retrieved 6 April 2010.

^ "Anger over Dutch Srebrenica medal". BBC News. 4 December 2006. Retrieved 8 January 2007.

^ Karacs, Imre (3 June 2007). "Serb war-crimes arrest puts EU talks back on the agenda". The Times (London). Archived from the original on 13 August 2008. Retrieved 4 June 2007.

^ "ICTY, "The Cases", Zdravko Tolimir. Retrieved 25 July 2010". Icty.org. Retrieved 26 May 2011.

^ "Bosnian Serb Zdravko Tolimir convicted over Srebrenica". BBC News. 12 December 2012. Retrieved 13 December 2012.

^ "Serbia captures fugitive Karadzic". BBC News. 21 July 2008. Retrieved 21 July 2008.

^ ICTY Karadzic case information sheet http://www.un.org/icty/cases-e/cis/karadzic/CIS-Karadzic.pdf

^ "Radovan Karadzic: The charges". BBC News. 23 October 2009. Retrieved 20 April 2010.

^ "ICTY Cases, Radovan Karadžić. Retrieved 25 July 2010". Icty.org. Retrieved 26 May 2011.

^ "EP: 11 July to be Srebrenica remembrance day" Archived 24 January 2009 at the Wayback Machine., B92. Retrieved 16 January 2008.

^ "Za RS neprihvatljivo obilježavanje 11. jula" Archived 18 January 2009 at the Wayback Machine., Sarajevo-x. Retrieved 16 January 2008.

^ "Serbian MPs offer apology for Srebrenica massacre". BBC News. 31 March 2010. Retrieved 31 March 2010.

^ "Serbia apologizes for Srebrenica massacre". CBC News. 31 March 2010. Retrieved 31 March 2010.

^ "Declaration represents distancing from crimes". B92.net. Archived from the original on 26 September 2011. Retrieved 26 May 2011.

^ "Tihić: Sad i BiH mora donijeti deklaraciju kojom će osuditi zločine nad Srbima i Hrvatima". Otvoreno.ba. Archived from the original on 6 July 2011. Retrieved 26 May 2011.

^ "Serbia president 'apologises' for massacre". aljazeera.com.

^ "Envoy slams Bosnia Serbs for questioning Srebrenica". Reuters. 21 April 2010. Retrieved 21 April 2010.

^ "RS Government Special Session A Distasteful Attempt to Question Genocide". OHR. 21 April 2010. Archived from the original on 18 March 2015. Retrieved 21 April 2010.

^ a b Srebrenica massacre 'not genocide', The Sydney Morning Herald/Agence France-Presse, 13 July 2010

^ van de Bildt, Joyce, "Srebrenica: A Dutch national trauma", Journal of Peace, Conflict & Development, Issue 21, March 2015. ISSN 1742-0601. (Retrieved 14 July 2015). http://www.bradford.ac.uk/ssis/peace-conflict-and-development/

^ Boon, Kristen. "Supreme Court Decision Rendered in Dutchbat Case: the Netherlands Responsible" 31 Aug — 6 September 2013. "Opinio Juris" website. (Retrieved 15 July 2015) http://opiniojuris.org/2013/09/06/supreme-court-decision-srebrenica-massacre-netherlands-responsible/

^ "Dutch state liable for three Srebrenica deaths - court", BBC Website, 6 September 2013. (Retrieved 14 July 2015). http://www.bbc.co.uk/news/world-europe-23986063

^ Bilefsky, Dan; Sengupta, Somini (8 July 2015). "Srebrenica Massacre, After 20 Years, Still Casts a Long Shadow in Bosnia". The New York Times.

^ "Russia blocks U.N. condemnation of Srebrenica as a genocide". Reuters. 8 July 2015.

^ "613 Srebrenica Victims to be Buried at a Memorial Ceremony in Potočari". Ic-mp.org. Retrieved 11 July 2012.

^ "Bridging the Gap in Srebrenica, Bosnia and Herzegovina". ICTY. Retrieved 20 April 2010.

^ "Hague Justice Portal, "Srebrenica in summary – An overview of the legal proceedings relating to the 1995 genocide". Retrieved 31 July 2010". Haguejusticeportal.net. Retrieved 26 May 2011.

^ Rod Nordland (13 August 2001). "Crimes Against Humanity". Newsweek. Retrieved 20 April 2010.

^ ICTY. "Prosecutor vs Krstic, Appeals Chamber Judgement". United Nations. 19 April 2004. para. No. 37. (PDF) http://web.archive.org/web/20090326134340/http://www.un.org/icty/krstic/Appeal/judgement/krs-aj040419e.pdf. Archived from the original (PDF) on 26 March 2009. Retrieved 11 July 2012. Missing or empty |title= (help) PDF (700 KB)

^ "ICTY: The prosecutor of the tribunal against Slobodan Milosevic – Amended Indictment". United Nations. 5 March 2007. Archived from the original on 7 March 2004. Retrieved 26 May 2011.

^ "Popovic et al. 'Srebrenica' Trial to Begin on 14 July 2006". ICTY. 11 July 2006. Retrieved 10 June 2010.

^ "Seven convicted over 1995 Srebrenica massacre". CNN. 10 June 2010.

^ Roumeliotis, Greg (10 September 2010). "Bosnian Serbs could face new Srebrenica war crimes trial". Reuters.

^ "Summary of the Judgement in the Case of Prosecutor v. Momčilo Perišić" (PDF). The Hague: International Criminal Tribunal for the former Yugoslavia. 6 September 2011. Retrieved 7 September 2011.

^ "PERISIC SENTENCED TO 27 YEARS FOR CRIMES IN BH AND CROATIA". The Hague: Sense-Agency. 6 September 2011. Retrieved 7 September 2011.

^ "Bosnian Serb War Crimes Fugitive on His Way to the Hague" Archived 4 June 2007 at the Wayback Machine., VOA News (1 June 2007). Retrieved 31 July 2008.

^ "Tolimir Requested Use of Chemical Weapons in Zepa" Archived 8 October 2007 at the Wayback Machine., SENSE Tribunal (22 August 2006). Retrieved 31 July 2008.

^ BBC News, 1 June 2007 [40]. Retrieved 8 April 2010.

^ BalkanInsight.com, 26 February 2010 http://web.archive.org/web/20100228024232/http://www.balkaninsight.com:80 /en/main/news/26147/. Archived from the original on 28 February 2010. Retrieved 8 April 2010. Missing or empty |title= (help). Retrieved 8 April 2010.

^ "Ratko Mladic arrested: Bosnia war crimes suspect held". BBC. 26 May 2011. Retrieved 26 May 2011.

^ "Q&A – Karadzic's legal position" [dead link] BBC News

^ "Radovan Karadzic refuses to enter plea at the Hague" The Times

^ "Karadzic says defence 'not ready'." Al Jazeera

^ Prosecutor's Marked-up Indictment, ICTY Case No. IT-95-5/18-PT THE PROSECUTOR v RADOVAN KARADZIC, 19 October 2009. Retrieved 7 June 2011

^ Prosecutor's Marked-up Indictment, ICTY Case No. IT-09-92-I THE PROSECUTOR v RATKO MLADIC, 1 June 2011. Retrieved 7 June 2011

^ Hudson, Alexandra (26 February 2007). "Serbia cleared of genocide, failed to stop killing", Reuters. Retrieved 31 July 2008.

^ ICJ press release 2007/8 26 February 2007, See points 7 and 8

^ "ICJ: Summary of the Judgment of 26 February 2007 – Bosnia v. Serbia". Icj-cij.org. 11 July 1996. Retrieved 26 May 2011.

^ Simons, Marlise (27 February 2007). "Court Declares Bosnia Killings Were Genocide", The New York Times. Retrieved 31 July 2008.

^ Simons, Marlise (9 April 2007). "Genocide Court Ruled for Serbia Without Seeing Full War Archive", The New York Times. Retrieved 31 July 2008.

^ Clifford, Lisa (20 April 2007). "Del Ponte Denies Belgrade Deal Claims", Institute for War & Peace Reporting. Retrieved 31 July 2008.

^ Peric Zimonjic, Vesna (11 April 2007). "Serb 'Scorpions' guilty of Srebrenica massacre" Archived 30 September 2007 at the Wayback Machine., The Independent. Retrieved 31 July 2008.

^ "Hague Tribunal Transfers Trbic Case to Bosnian Court" Archived 13 June 2007 at the Wayback Machine., VOA News (11 June 2008). Retrieved 31 July 2008.

^ The Court of Bosnia and Herzegovina – Trbic case: Charged with genocide pursuant to Article 171 of the Criminal Code of Bosnia and Herzegovina (CC BiH) in conjunction with the killing members of the group, causing serious bodily or mental harm to members of the group, deliberately inflicting on the group conditions of life calculated to bring about its physical destruction in whole or in part, imposing measures intended to prevent births within the group (X-KR-07/386 – Trbic Milorad)

^ a b c d e f g h i j k l The Court of Bosnia and Herzegovina – Mitrovic and others (Kravice) – Accused of the criminal offence of genocide in violation of Article 171 of the Criminal Code of Bosnia and Herzegovina (X-KR-05/24 – Mitrovic and others (Kravice)).

^ a b c d e f g h i j k l m n Aida Cerkez-Robinson (2008-07-30). "7 Bosnian Serbs guilty of genocide in Srebrenica". USA Today. Archived from the original on 2016-02-17.

^ a b c d e f g h i j k l m n "Bosnian Serbs jailed for genocide". BBC News. 29 July 2008. Retrieved 29 July 2008.

^ Radosavljevic, Zoran (20 April 2010). "Croatia arrests suspect in Srebrenica massacre". Reuters. Retrieved 20 April 2010.

^ a b c "Vlastimir Golijan Pleads Guilty to Genocide". Balkan Investigative Reporting Network. 8 September 2010. Archived from the original on 15 September 2010.

^ a b "Suspect Marko Boškić Extradited To BiH". The Prosecutor's Office of Bosnia and Herzegovina. 29 April 2010. Retrieved 6 May 2010.

^ a b "Israel arrests suspect in Srebrenica massacre". CNN. 18 January 2011.

^ Corder, Mike; Cerkez, Aida (18 January 2011). "Israel arrests man wanted in Srebrenica massacre". Associated Press.[dead link]

^ Service, Haaretz (18 January 2011). "Israeli man arrested for alleged involvement in Bosnia genocide – Israel News | Haaretz Daily Newspaper". Haaretz. Retrieved 5 February 2013.

^ "Israel to extradite Bosnian Serb over Srebrenica massacre – Israel News | Haaretz Daily Newspaper". Haaretz. Reuters. 2 August 2011. Retrieved 5 February 2013.

^ Jeremy, Yonah (29 November 2012). "Court: Extradite Serb-Israeli wanted for... JPost – National News". The Jerusalem Post. Retrieved 5 February 2013.

^ a b "Police Arrest Bozidar Kuvelja for Alleged Involvement in Genocide". Balkan Investigative Reporting Network. 18 January 2011. Archived from the original on 22 July 2011.

^ "Two genocide suspects arrested in BiH, Israel". Southeast European Times. 19 January 2011.

^ Milorad Trbic Found Guilty of Genocide Archived 29 March 2010 at the Wayback Machine. 16 October 2009

^ a b "Two Bosnian Serbs Jailed For 31 Years Over Srebrenica". The New York Times. 22 April 2010. Retrieved 22 April 2010.[dead link]

^ "Marko Boškić sentenced to 10 years imprisonment". Court of Bosnia & Herzegovina. 19 June 2010.

^ "Radovan Karadzic, a Bosnian Serb, Gets 40 Years Over Genocide and War Crimes". The New York Times. Retrieved 24 March 2016.

^ a b "Bosnian Serbs jailed for Srebrenica warehouse killings". Euronews. 25 May 2012.[dead link]

^ a b c d "Srebrenica: 142 Years of Prison For Branjevo Crimes". Balkan Insight. 15 June 2012.

^ "Former Bosnian Serb police officer sentenced for Srebrenica war crimes". Southeast European Times. 15 May 2011.

^ "Bosnian Serb cleared of genocide". BBC. 6 May 2010. Retrieved 6 May 2010.

^ a b "Duško Jević et al. Verdict". Court of Bosnia and Herzegovina. 25 May 2012.

^ "US deports man sought for war crimes to Bosnia". Fox News Channel. 24 May 2012.

^ a b "Two Serbian citizens indicted for Srebrenica crime". B82. 15 June 2012. Archived from the original on 17 June 2012.

^ "Srebrenica :: Introduction to the Case Srebrenica :: Van Diepen Van der Kroef". Vandiepen.com. 11 July 1995. Retrieved 26 May 2011.

^ Gottlied, Sebastian (18 June 2008). "Srebrenica genocide testcase for UN immunity" Archived 20 December 2008 at the Wayback Machine., Radio Netherlands Worldwide. Retrieved 31 July 2008.

^ The Hague District Court; Writ of Summons Archived 25 June 2008 at the Wayback Machine., The Hague, p. 198

^ The Hague District Court; Judgment in the incidental proceedings, The Hague, 10 July 2008

^ Corder, Mike (10 July 2008). "Dutch Court rules in Srebrenica Civil Suit"[dead link], Associated Press. Retrieved 31 July 2008.

^ F. V. (30 October 2008). "Advokatski tim podnio žalbu" Archived 26 December 2008 at the Wayback Machine., Dnevniavaz.ba. Retrieved 30 October 2008.

^ Srebrenica lawsuit against Holland opens Archived 7 June 2011 at the Wayback Machine., B92, 17 June 2008

^ a b District Court hears Srebrenica cases, The Hague Justice Portal, 18 June 2008

^ The Hague Justice Portal DomClic Project, "Nuhanović vs The Netherlands". Retrieved 5 August 2010.

^ "Nederlandse Staat aansprakelijk voor dood drie Moslimmannen na val Srebrenica". rechtspraak.nl. Archived from the original on 18 March 2012. Retrieved 11 July 2012.

^ "State responsible for death of three Muslim men in Srebrenica". Rechtspraak.nl. 6 September 2013. Archived from the original on 11 September 2013.

^ Huiskamp, Frank (6 September 2013). "Kabinet zal handelen naar uitspraak Hoge Raad over Srebrenica" (in Dutch). NRC.

^ ICTY; "Address by ICTY President Theodor Meron, at Potocari Memorial Cemetery" The Hague, 23 June 2004 https://web.archive.org/web/20121017124026/http://www.un.org/icty/pressreal/2004/p860-e.htm. Archived from the original on 17 October 2012. Retrieved 27 May 2008. Missing or empty |title= (help)

^ ICJ; The Application of the Convention on the Prevention and Punishment of the Crime of Genocide (Bosnia and Herzegovina v. Serbia and Montenegro), case 91, The Hague, 26 February 2007, p. 108, paragraph 297. [41]

^ "Report of the Secretary-General pursuant to General Assembly resolution 53/35—The Fall of Srebrenica" [42][dead link]

^ "Report of the Secretary-General pursuant to General Assembly resolution 53/35—The Fall of Srebrenica" paragraph 476 [43][dead link]

^ "Report of the Secretary-General pursuant to General Assembly resolution 53/35—The Fall of Srebrenica" paragraph 478 [44][dead link]

^ a b "Report of the Secretary-General pursuant to General Assembly resolution 53/35—The Fall of Srebrenica" paragraph 479". United Nations. Retrieved 21 July 2015.[dead link]

^ a b c Ivanisevic, Bogdan. "Oric's Two Years", Human Rights Watch. Retrieved 31 July 2008.

^ a b c d "ICTY Weekly Press Briefing, July 2005". United Nations. 5 March 2007. Archived from the original on 10 May 2009. Retrieved 26 May 2011.

^ a b c RDC. "The Myth Of Bratunac: A Blatant Numbers Game" Archived 8 May 2009 at the Wayback Machine.

^ Sadovic, Merdijana (4 November 2005). "Courtside: Oric", Institute for War and Peace Reporting. Retrieved 31 July 2008.

^ "Bosnian Congress—census 1991—Northeast of Bosnia". Hdmagazine.com. Archived from the original on 11 July 2011. Retrieved 26 May 2011.

^ "VRS, "Warpath of the Bratunac brigade", cited in: RDC. "The Myth Of Bratunac: A Blatant Numbers Game"". Archived from the original on 22 December 2010. Retrieved 22 December 2010.[dead link]

^ Florence Hartmann, Spokesperson for the Office of the Prosecutor, ICTY Weekly Press Briefing, 6 July 2005 http://web.archive.org/web/20090510013827/http://www.un.org:80/icty/briefin

g/2005/PB050706.htm. Archived from the original on 10 May 2009. Retrieved 26 May 2011. Missing or empty |title= (help)

^ ICTY: Naser Orić verdict Archived 3 March 2009 at the Wayback Machine.

^ Heil, Rebekah (23 June 2007). "Bosnia's "Book of the Dead"", Institute for War & Peace Reporting. Retrieved 31 July 2008.

^ RDC Norway Archived 19 July 2007 at the Wayback Machine.—The Bosnian Book of Dead (short analysis)

^ Serbs accuse world of ignoring their suffering, AKI, 13 July 2006

^ J.C.H. Blom et al. (2002) NIOD Report: Srebrenica. Reconstruction, background, consequences and analyses of the fall of a Safe Area (Appendix IV, History and Reminders in East Bosnia)

^ ICTY Weekly Press Briefing, 14 March 2007 – ICTY spokesperson describes "Licna karta Srebrenice" ("Srebrenica Identity Card") by Milivoje Ivanisevic as shameful denial and relativisation of facts about the Srebrenica genocide established beyond reasonable doubt by the Court. Retrieved 21 March 2011

^ ICTY Outreach Programme, "Facts about Srebrenica", A Planned Killing Operation, p 6, undated – after June 2005 [45]. Retrieved 8 April 2010.

^ Supreme Court Judgement, ibid. p7 para x

^ Supreme Court Judgement, ibid. p12

^ "The fall of Srebrenica". Netherlands Institute for War Documentation. p. Part III chapter 9.6. Retrieved 2013-04-10.

^ a b Andreas Arnseth. "Norsk oberst får kritikk etter folkemord". VG.

^ a b c d e "– Forsøker å skjule sannheten". Ny Tid. 24 September 2005. Archived from the original on 22 February 2014.

^ "Srebrenica: Part 3, Chapter 6, Section 3".

^ Styrken som sviktet[dead link]

^ Ian Traynor (19 March 2010). "US general: Gay Dutch soldiers caused Srebrenica massacre". The Guardian (UK). Retrieved 3 June 2011.

^ "General Sheehan: gays responsible for Srebrenica massacre". YouTube. Retrieved 26 May 2011.

^ "Former US general: 'gays make Dutch military weak'". NRC Handelsblad. Retrieved 3 June 2011.

^ Ian Traynor (19 March 2010). "US general: Gay Dutch soldiers caused Srebrenica massacre". The Guardian (UK). Retrieved 26 May 2011.

^ Foreign, Our (19 March 2010). "Gay Dutch soldiers responsible for Srebrenica massacre says US general". The Daily Telegraph (UK). Retrieved 26 May 2011.

^ "PM slams 'disgraceful' Srebrenica gay comments". Javno.com. 19 March 2010. Retrieved 26 May 2011.[dead link]

^ "Dutch fury at US general's gay theory over Srebrenica". BBC News. 19 March 2010. Retrieved 26 May 2011.

^ O'Keefe, Ed. "Ex-General Apologizes for Dutch Gay Soldier Remark." The Washington Post. 31 March 2010.

^ a b "- Stoltenberg har medansvar for Srebrenica". Aftenposten.

^ Denial of genocide – on the possibility of normalising relations in the region by Sonja Biserko (the Helsinki Committee for Human Rights in Serbia) and Edina Bečirević (Faculty of Criminalistics, Criminology and Security Studies of the University of Sarajevo).

^ Alternative Views

Report of Srebrenica Research Group, alleged that "the contention that as many as 8,000 Muslims were killed has no basis in available evidence and is essentially a political construct".

Report of International Strategic Studies Association (ISSA), claimed that the "alleged casualty number of 7,000 victims [is] vastly inflated and unsupported by evidence"

The real story behind Srebrenica by the former UNPROFOR commander, Gen. Lewis MacKenzie, The Globe and Mail, 14 July 2005.

"The Forbidden Srebrenica report", report denying the Srebrenica massacre issued by the Republika Srpska Bureau for Cooperation with the ICTY in September 2002.

The Politics of the Srebrenica Massacre article argues that only some Bosniaks were executed, most died in battle, and some of the bodies in mass graves are actually Serbs, by Edward S. Herman, 7 July 2005

^ Armatta, Judith (27 February 2003)."Milosevic's Propaganda War", Institute of War & Peace Reporting. Retrieved 31 July 2008.

^ "ICTY Indictment of Milosevic, clause 25, section g". United Nations. 5 March 2007. Archived from the original on 7 March 2004. Retrieved 26 May 2011.

^ Bennett, Christopher. "how yugoslavia's destroyers harnessed the media", Frontline. Retrieved 31 July 2008.

^ EXPERT REPORT OF RENAUD DE LA BROSSE "Political Propaganda and the Plan to Create 'A State For All Serbs:' Consequences of using media for ultra-nationalist ends", paragraph 74

^ Vulliamy, Ed (30 April 2005). "After the massacre, a homecoming". The Guardian (London).

^ Sullivan, Stacy (5 July 2005). "The Wall of Denial". Institute for War & Peace Reporting.

^ "Srebrenica was not genocide: Bosnian Serb leader". Agence France-Presse. 27 April 2010. Archived from the original on 17 July 2010. Retrieved 28 April 2010.

^ Arslanagic, Sabina (3 December 2010). "Dodik Again Denies Srebrenica Genocide". Balkan Insight.

^ "Serbian president denies Srebrenica genocide". The Guardian (London). 2 June 2012.

^ "Rights group sues paper for Bosnia genocide denial". Associated Press. 19 April 2010. Retrieved 19 April 2010.[dead link]

^ "Srebrenica Research Group – Group members and mission". Srebrenica-report.com. Archived from the original on 24 March 2008. Retrieved 13 July 2015.

^ Quoted in International Strategic Studies Association – Special Report Srebrenica Controversy Becomes Increasingly Politicized ISSA Special Report – Balkan Strategic Studies, 19 September 2003

^ MacKenzie (ret'd) Archived 3 February 2010 at the Wayback Machine.. Jmss.org. Retrieved 13 August 2010.

^ "Balkan Witness – General Lewis MacKenzie". Glypx.com. Retrieved 13 August 2010.

^ and includes UN former officials, journalists see http://srebrenica-deconstructed.com/people.htm.

^ "Srebrenica And the Politics of War Crimes - conclusions". Srebrenica Research Group. Retrieved 19 July 2015.

^ Schabas, William (18 September 2000). Genocide in International Law: The Crime of Crimes. Cambridge University Press. pp. 175–200, 201. ISBN 0-521-78790-4. Retrieved 16 May 2009.

^ "Bauer: U Srebrenici je bilo masovno ubistvo, a ne genocide" [Srebrenica was Mass Murder, not Genocide] (in Serbian). RTRS. 29 June 2015.

^ "Nazi hunter: Comparing Srebrenica and Holocaust is "absurd"". B92. 17 June 2015.

Other References

Michas, Takis (2002). Unholy Alliance: Greece and Milosevic's Serbia in the Nineties. Texas A&M University Press. ISBN 1-58544-183-X.

Ramet, Sabrina P. (2006). The Three Yugoslavias: State-Building And Legitimation, 1918–2005. Indiana University Press. ISBN 0-253-34656-8.

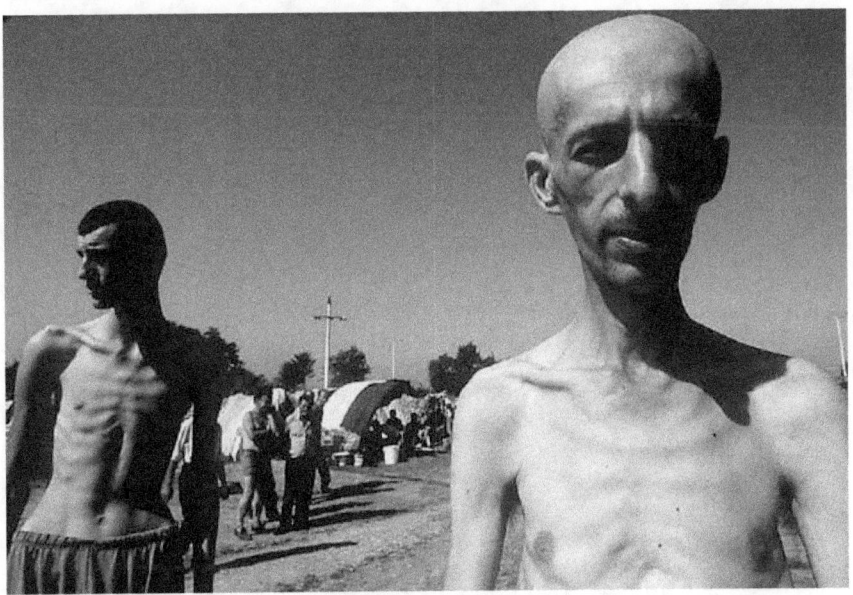

Bosniak civilians in Serb-run Trnopolje concentration camp in August 1992

Bosniak (Bosnian Muslim) civilians the notorious Serb-run Maniaca concentration camp in north-west Bosnia, near Prijedor, in August of 1992, during the Bosnian Genocide.

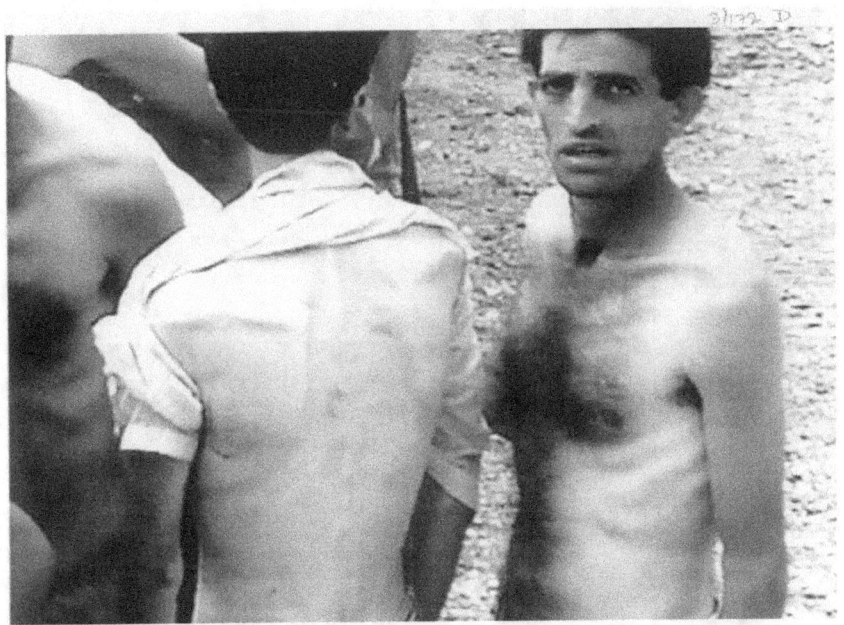

Tortured, beaten, and emaciated Bosniak (Bosnian Muslim) men in the Trnopolje concentration camp near Prijedor, north-west Bosnia, during the Bosnian Genocide.

Bosnian Genocide, August 1992. Sign (visible from Center to Left) written in cyrillic letters reads MINES. Manjaca concentration camp near Prijedor, north-west Bosnia. The camp was surrounded by mines to prevent escape of prisoners. Thousands of civilians, mostly Bosniaks (Bosnian Muslims) were tortured and killed there.

Manjaca concentration camp near Prijedor, north-west Bosnia in August 1992. Thousands of civilians, mostly Bosniaks (Bosnian Muslims) were tortured and killed there.

Srebrenica massacre: Budak mass grave, Kamenica 9, where some of 8,372 Srebrenica genocide victims had been dumped after systematic killings in July 1995.

Srebrenica massacre: Budak mass grave, Kamenica 9, where some of 8,372 Srebrenica genocide victims had been dumped after systematic killings in July 1995.

www.ingramcontent.com/pod-product-compliance
Lightning Source LLC
Chambersburg PA
CBHW070256190526
45169CB00001B/430